JUN 1 1 2017

9-22-17(4)

D1595206

NEW NORDIC GARDENS

NEW NORDIC GARDENS

Scandinavian Landscape Design

Annika Zetterman

With 291 illustrations

Thames & Hudson

Front cover: Plumes of
calamagrostis brachytricha
in a garden in Sealand,
Denmark, by Tidens
Staduer Design.

Back cover (clockwise from
top left): The ornamental
grass *Miscanthus*.
A garden by Østengen &
Bergo Landskapsarkitekter
in Oslo, Norway.
A stone path in a garden by
DesignHaver in Funen,
Denmark.
A garden by Zetterman
Garden Design in Värmdö,
Stockholm.
Sumac trees in a garden in
Oslo, Norway.
Heritage plant *Lilium
martagon.*

p.2: A planting scheme in
a garden in Saltsjö Duvnäs,
Sweden, by Zetterman
Garden Design.

p.7: Ice formations near
Stockholm, Sweden.

p.8: *Rhododendron
catawbiense* "Lee's
Dark Purple."

Text © 2017 Annika Zetterman
New Nordic Gardens © 2017 Thames & Hudson
Ltd, London

First published in 2017 in the United States of America
by Thames & Hudson Inc., 500 Fifth Avenue, New York,
New York 10110

www.thamesandhudsonusa.com

Library of Congress Control Number 2016943102

ISBN 978-0-500-51945-5

Printed and bound in China by Reliance Printing
(Shen Zhen) Co., Ltd.

Take a piece of ice in your hand and find our culture in it;
find it in a stone smoothed by the rapids, or in sand that
waves have shaped...

Tapio Wirkkala, Finnish designer and sculptor (1915–1985)

INTRODUCTION

Scandinavia is a region that is geographically isolated in many respects, and is often sparsely populated and quiet. Its silent gardens have in recent years undergone major transformation, and are now viewed as a great asset. Scandinavians themselves tend to be modest souls with sometimes rustic backgrounds, living in countries that have undergone rapid development in modern times, swiftly becoming advanced and worldly societies. With shared values, democracies and idiosyncrasies we cultivate our heritage as design nations, and are proud of our progress. We love to use raw and bare materials. We marry functionality and sustainability with grace. We embrace all things natural and simple.

Scandinavian design is renowned worldwide: comprising work carried out with a high level of attention to functionality and quality, and based on philosophies of modesty and equality. The term encompasses an entire movement in creative production that emerged from the five Nordic countries (Denmark, Finland, Iceland, Norway and Sweden) in the mid-twentieth century, a period sometimes referred to as the 'Golden Age', the legacy of which endures in Scandinavia.

Today's generation of skilled designers in Scandinavia look on our design heritage as a strength. The book shows examples of how we are influenced by our past, but also how gardens are now being created that push boundaries and innovate. In recent years garden design has gone beyond the typical perception of pale, tame and neutral, with garden designers sometimes adopting a more daring and resolute – yet still elegant – approach. Each chapter of this book explains one distinct characteristic of Scandinavian design, showing how this characteristic is applied in contemporary garden designs and outdoor compositions. The book showcases a wide range of images of outdoor spaces created by skilled garden designers, landscape architects and architects across Scandinavia. A description accompanies each image, explaining its significance in the context of the chapter.

Furthermore, the book describes fundamental notions of how to make a composition visually interesting, illustrated with examples. In any garden it is vital to get a sense of the space, in order to achieve a pleasing and genuine end result. The space within a garden should be organized in a logical and practical way, enabling it to be useful and readily enjoyed. Gardens that connect with their surroundings, and with art and architecture, can be very successful – but ultimately, design principles are applied to prompt emotion and to stir our feelings.

The characteristics of Scandinavia – how our particular mentality and rural heritage is translated and reflected – can be found in all aspects of a garden. The implementation of hard landscaping is one of the elements where this can be seen. We see beauty in the bare and the exposed, and treat materials with the utmost respect. The definition of sustainability, a word widely used today, has always been fundamental to Scandinavian identity. We had to work hard in a harsh environment, and everything had to be made to last.

From the barren landscapes of Iceland, over the roaring mountains of Norway, into the deepest forests of Finland, on to the sweeping meadows of Sweden, down to the sandy soils of Denmark – Scandinavia is vast. Weather and climate are therefore discussed broadly and in general terms. In Scandinavia we create gardens in order to communicate with our landscapes, the silent spaces of the north. Nature itself gives rise to incredible artistic expression and there is much that we can learn from it.

With seasonal variation comes opportunity, and the book provides an understanding of how gardens change with the seasons in the north. Parts of Scandinavia experience dramatic weather changes. We constantly work between hope and despair, always in anticipation of what is to come. We experience distinct seasons, with comfortably warm summers and cold, snowy winters, and we celebrate them. By virtue of experiencing so many variations, sometimes in extremes, gardens in Scandinavia are constantly changing, too. Natural light evolves with the seasons, in the north especially, and this is shown in the endless colour changes in a garden. Making use of the seasons as a creative tool, together with fundamental notions of composition, enables Scandinavian gardens to be exciting, aesthetically pleasing and always evoking new feelings.

Soft landscaping and planting is important in gardens, protecting both people and wildlife, giving pleasure and fostering a sense of well-being. Climate and soil determine what grows, however, and the options are very different throughout Scandinavia depending on the particular conditions. However, every garden offers plentiful opportunities to make a useful and inviting space. Ornamental grasses are among the most versatile plants in Scandinavia, and these can be used in many inventive ways, as shown in the book. Cultivating the soil is in our genes – it is what enabled us to survive in our environment. And, taking into account the current trend for leading an active, healthy lifestyle and our passionate views on food, the book also discusses the function of gardens in this context.

Here you will discover that our past informs our future. Our societies are faced with complex environmental challenges, in which the flow of resources needs to be addressed. Roof gardens and greenery are important both to people and the cities they inhabit, not only aesthetically, but also for protection. Equally, the use of reclaimed materials and environmentally friendly approaches in garden design is essential to ensure a sustainable future.

The Scandinavian countries differ from each other in certain respects, but the common way of life, the democratic principles and the sense of community spirit run through them all. The book shows examples of communal gardens, playgrounds filled with vitality and landscapes made for people to socialize, integrate and participate in the space. Put simply, gardens are important to people. Many of us lead hectic lives, surrounded by gadgets and devices intended to make the day more efficient. But living life in the fast lane can lead people to long for escape, to places free from stress. The book shows highly creative examples of spaces laid out for people to enjoy, gardens that motivate and memorable places where the senses can be awakened.

The gardens that we create stay with us for decades to come and should therefore enchant us from the start. They should help us, our wildlife and our wider environment to thrive. They should be designed with dignity, and worked on with modesty and maintained with persistence. This is how we think, how we work, and this is what we are.

Year-round interest
—
Opposite: Careful garden planning enables a striking display all through the year. This *Scabiosa ochroleuca*, in a garden in Vallentuna, Sweden, provides winter elegance with its slender branches and buttons, the interlinking stems supporting one another and creating visual interest. Its cream colour in summer may provide a burst of vitality, but in the enchanting northern light it remains uplifting and optimistic even in the coldest months.

NOTE
The term 'Scandinavia' is generally used when referring to Denmark, Norway and Sweden only, while the term 'Nordic' also includes Finland and Iceland. In this book, however, as is common when discussing architecture and design, 'Scandinavia' refers to Denmark, Finland, Iceland, Norway and Sweden.

SIMPLE

Scandinavian design values and basic principles

Simplicity might be the first word that comes to mind when asked to define Scandinavian design. It underlies a common set of values and beliefs shared across Scandinavia, and makes us think about the essence of what we create, leading to a result that is genuine, pure and modest. However, the term also implies a certain complexity in the treatment of materials, how function marries with sparse detailing, that leads to what we perceive as sophistication – and perfection.

Designed gardens and landscapes are by nature complex; this is how we imbue a space with meaning, character and soul. Consequently simplicity in Scandinavian garden design doesn't equate to achieving quick results, taking short-cuts or merely subtracting clutter. The priority is always careful execution and high-quality results. With this simple expression every element has meaning, adding significance to the design. In the end simplicity is about being direct and working with materials in an honest way; turning every single stone in a dry stone wall to show its best side.

Design in nature
—
When strolling around a summer garden in Scandinavia, you may notice free-flowing planting of fruit trees and berries. Hidden beneath foliage like butterfly wings, you might encounter dangling clusters of gooseberries just waiting to be picked, like these in Dalarna, Sweden. Taking a bunch into your palm, you will see nature's own design perfection: the saturation of green, the perfect oval shape and the wonderful texture, like a mesh of delicate stripes or the veins in a hand.

The 'Golden Age' of Scandinavian design

Scandinavian design is renowned all over the world. The term represents a movement of creative production that emerged in the five Nordic countries (Denmark, Finland, Iceland, Norway and Sweden) in the mid-20th century. During this period, sometimes referred to as the 'Golden Age', Scandinavian design was based on philosophies of functionality, modesty and equality, and this legacy has endured in Scandinavia. Numerous outstanding designers and architects now considered icons, such as Arne Jacobsen, Bruno Mathsson, Alvar Aalto, Verner Panton and Hans Wegner, were working at the height of the Scandinavian design era.

The years following the Second World War were filled with optimism, although people were still living in rudimentary circumstances and in a harsh climate. During these tough times it was important to foster a caring environment, and design efficiency was paramount in achieving this. Construction had to last, and everyday objects were made not only to be functional and delightful and to solve a problem, but also to be affordable to the masses. Although new materials such as plastics – ideally suited to mass production – were introduced at this time, more traditional natural materials such as wood remained central to the Scandinavian ethos, and still are today.

Design inspired by nature

In Scandinavia it is viewed as a privilege to be close to nature, and we have an enormous respect for our surroundings – the forests, lakes, fields and mountains. We are born and raised close to nature, acquiring knowledge of how to treat our surroundings and how to respect and care about the wild. In general nature fascinates Scandinavians, and we have long been

concerned with interpreting how it affects our emotions and moods. Not only do designers and architects take a sustainable approach, but often they choose to take direct inspiration from, or communicate in some way with, nature through their creations. As an example, Finnish designer and sculptor Tapio Wirkkala created a platter inspired by a leaf and a vase inspired by ice, while Danish architect Arne Jacobsen gave organic-influenced names to his work, such as the chairs 'Ant', 'Lily' and 'Drop'. Nature-inspired work can be found throughout history, in historic as well as in more modern times. Floral patterns have made their mark on classic design fabrics such as 'Unikko', by Marimekko, and 'Primavera', created by Svenskt Tenn. Current designers are likewise being praised for their imaginative creations inspired by nature, plants and our abundant wildlife.

A Scandinavian garden

Today's generation of skilled designers in Scandinavia look at our design heritage and the Golden Age as an asset and a model for developing creations, but also reach further back in history. They appreciate native plants and natural materials, some dating back thousands of years, such as common elder and apples, used by the Vikings, as well as natural stone, granite, limestone and slate. By blending new ideas with those from our past we can push creative boundaries, while our attitude stays the same: to create long-lasting gardens and to cherish our common ethos, history and culture. A modern garden may be enclosed by a traditional dry stone wall, a hedge or a wooden fence, old or new. Dry stone walls were once common in southern parts of Scandinavia, where wood was not readily available and cobbles and stones were removed from agrarian land, while

Respect for the environment
—

Sustainability is an intrinsic part of our heritage in Scandinavia, echoing through our buildings and the surrounding landscape. This design intent embodies Iceland's respect for the environment, where the existing vegetation surrounding this property in Kiðjaberg, by Minarc, has been carefully retained. The garden and house seem to communicate throughout the space, with gravel used to enhance the naturalistic look and contrast with the solid panels of the house. A timber walkway leading to the entrance employs fine lines that run towards the house to invite the visitor inside.

15

*The influence of
functionalism*
—
Typical Scandinavian
design is both functional
and sparse. This
classic chair design
by Grythyttan Stålmöbler
and Artur Lindqvist
has been made in a
village deep in the
forests of Bergslagen
in Sweden since 1930.
The original aim was
to produce functional
and durable furniture
made from wood and
steel. The craftsmanship
has been passed down
the generations and the
ethos remains the same:
only using the best
stocks of wood, sawn for
maximum stability and
employing sustainable
production processes.

gardens in the north were often marked by a wooden fence of round poles made of spruce or juniper, as seen in Finland, Norway and Sweden. Natural stone in large quantities, with sizes and surface textures not available in the past, can be seen in gardens today, and nurseries offer a wide selection of plants. Taking an environmental approach we also consider heritage plants with cultural resonances, and meadows for biodiversity, sometimes including green sedum roofs in schemes. We stretch the seasons and make gardens useful all year round, incorporating water for cooling off in summer, fire pits in autumn and tranquil lighting in winter, only commonly seen until relatively recently in residential gardens.

When talking about gardens we often like to categorize them by style: woodland gardens, wildlife gardens, seaside gardens, city gardens and large country gardens to name but a few examples. Rather than thinking simply in terms of style, though,

remember that the most magnificent gardens have a soul; they express a particular atmosphere. Adding shingle to a seaside garden may seem natural, in consideration of the surroundings, but it will not automatically inspire. Rather it is the way the shingle is used in balance and in communication with other materials, and with soft landscaping such as ornamental grasses, that will awaken the senses. A garden with a soul is a place where you wish to be; it is a hidden sanctuary made to evoke powerful emotions. Scandinavian gardens therefore cross a range of styles depending on where the garden is situated, but all are based on our common value of simplicity we appreciate, using natural materials, sparse detailing and delicate planting.

A sense of space

Every design project has its own starting point; it can be an existing well-kept garden, an old and overgrown garden or a new plot of land – a blank canvas. In any garden the key is to get a sense of the space in order to achieve a pleasing end result. Before designing a garden you should view it from different angles, and get familiar with the terrain, the house (on site or on plan), the architecture and the people living there. Once you understand these parameters and the client's wishes and desires, the work of integrating ideas into a plan can start. Designing a garden is a problem-solving task as much as it is a creative process. Analysing the space will not only give you the dimensions you have to work with but should sow seeds of ideas and concepts for the design. Look at the garden as a place of opportunities and use levels, directions and interesting features to their advantage, enabling the process to be as creative, challenging and fun as possible. A mature tree can be excellent as a backdrop to a seating area, a boulder could make a fun focal point, and changing levels might create spaces with entirely different views from each other. The space of a garden should be organized in a logical and practical way so it is most useful and easily enjoyed, including for example easy, reliable access and comfortable, well-proportioned socializing areas.

Equally important when creating a garden design scheme is knowledge of soft and hard landscaping suited to the region, to create a unique, confident and location-appropriate garden. Familiarity with the local culture and customs of gardens, and the range of stones and wood available as well as soft materials, common plants, trees and perennials, will help you to adopt an honest and true approach, with a result that looks natural in its environment.

Designing a garden is a process, often involving sketching, reflection and a number of drafts and revisions before reaching the result. You may want to revisit the site to get to know the garden further and view your draft with a critical eye in order to get the very best out of the space. During the creative process you might approach the garden from one direction and then visualize it from a different angle in order to understand all its dimensions.

Every skilful garden designer or architect masters the art of reading and interpreting spaces, enabling evaluation of thoughts and elaborate concepts to achieve a satisfying composition. Whether you have an innate talent for design or not, you can always train your eye and improve. You can learn from closely observing the landscape as well as studying the work of expert designers. We can see fundamental notions of how to make a composition visually interesting in action around us every day – not only in gardens and landscapes – though we have to be careful not to miss them. Think, for example, of reading the newspaper in the morning – a well-executed layout makes it legible; walking down a street – where every façade shows consideration

Articulation through pattern

—

Patterns can be evocative and stimulate curiosity. The surface pattern of this garden floor in a design by Johan Sundberg Arkitektur in collaboration with Jessica Hallonsten, in Kämpinge, Sweden, shows rhythm in colour, flow and geometric structure. The aim was to create a lounge area with hints of the graceful and flamboyant styles of the Mediterranean. The framed area carries a distinctly different expression from the rest of the garden, setting up a strong contrast.

of detail, scale and proportion; or the plate of food served for dinner – an appetizing balance of colour, shape and texture.

Understanding basic rules of design will help in any successful scheme. It is essential for the creative process to balance these principles, though, or you may lose the essence of what you are creating, resulting in a garden that is neither useful nor aesthetically appealing. Design principles shouldn't take away from your composition, but should enhance it and give it meaning.

Basic design principles

Space

Space is a valuable asset, and should be treated with the very best of intentions. Majestic trees, barren rocks, areas of natural meadow and other existing elements can potentially be kept, providing natural flow, legacy and significance as part of the spatial scheme. A landscape

is formed of objects and space, referred to as mass and void. A garden without void therefore loses something of its essence. Void is the empty space that allows us to see objects, focuses our eye on details and gives us an understanding of the bigger picture. Objects have shapes and dimensions: length, width and height. When designing a garden we work with mass and void to break up the space, create perspectives and stimulate the imagination. Objects may also be interlinking or freestanding. For example, a circular object alone is freestanding, while several circles may be combined as a series of interlinking shapes.

Line

Line is the most fundamental geometric component in a space, and is a very powerful tool, leading the eye. A line can be straight or continuously bending in a curve. All lines have direction: horizontal, vertical or oblique. A line, while it is the

Combining formality and informality
—
Using formal and informal elements together is common in garden design. This garden by Østengen & Bergo Landskapsarkitekter in Oslo, Norway uses materials wisely, blending formality and informality through strict and resolute expressions in the hard landscaping, while the planting is more relaxed. The garden was designed to be gentle on the existing vegetation and habitats, which were not to be disturbed by the hard landscaping features in the slope.

most basic component, can create flow and movement across a surface. Straight lines are often perceived as direct and hard, in contrast to curved lines, which create organic shapes and appear soft and gentle to the eye. When designing a garden, combining straight and curved lines can provide interesting contrasts and variation in movement. How lines are used in the design scheme also has an emotional effect on what you communicate, whether sharp and determined, or caring and soft.

Balance

Balance gives a garden design stability. An unbalanced composition can lead to tension and is perceived as worrying to the eye. Balance involves the size and scale of objects, and the weight distribution in a design. In gardens balance gives us control not only of the shapes and objects but also the colour and texture of elements. Balance can be achieved in two ways, by symmetry or asymmetry, depending on the visual interest and mood that should be portrayed in the garden. Simply stated, in symmetry, weight distribution is exactly the same on each side of a central axis, with formal and sometimes static compositions as a result. Asymmetrical compositions are achieved by the variation of volumes on each side of an axis, such as several small objects to one side of an axis, balancing with one larger object on the other, potentially offering more variation and energy.

Scale and proportion

With scale and proportion we strive to set up communication between entities in the garden, and this will also determine how we feel when using and walking around the space. If there are many tall vertical structures we may feel small and enclosed in the space, while only very low objects can make us feel exposed. Using scale and proportion can attract attention and create interesting hierarchies in a garden, with objects complementing each other, rather

than fighting for attention. Consider that each entity in a garden has a size. How large or small elements are determines what relationship they have with each other, as well as the overall expression of the garden. Scale, proportion and size can be used as instruments to change the rhythm momentarily or to emphasize a feature. Deliberately over-sizing a column as a foundation to a static sculpture can prove rewarding, for example, to make it more prominent in the space.

Unity

Unity is the term used to explain the way that everything crystallizes and comes together, and is the mechanism by which the garden feels like one entity. It is achieved when the entire space has integrity and identity. Unity is dependent on many elements, which must be in agreement. Alignment and connection of objects, repetition and rhythm are all examples of techniques that together make a garden unified and send a message of consistency and cohesion across the space. Texture, pattern and colour are also factors that can bring unity to the garden.

Similarities and contrasts

In a design there is a purpose with every decision made, which follows the general idea and intentions for that space. By being selective in our choices and carefully planning how and where changes are made, relating to form, position, direction, structure, colour and texture, the garden can become more powerful in its expression. Contrasts and similarities should be considered across the scheme to maximize interest and attraction. Too many similarities in a space will make a garden uneventful. Large areas, such as a parking space or large patio, can look lifeless and sterile without any visual dynamics. Too many changes and contrasts, on the other hand, will make highlights disappear and the space may be rendered worrying to the eye and difficult to read.

Large windows link exterior and interior

—

The high standard of houses which we inhabit today tend to feature large windows to allow natural light to flood into the space. These also result in a natural connection with the garden, fostering an increased interest in what the immediate outdoor space has to offer, and how it communicates with the interior – as seen in this design by Johan Sundberg Arkitektur in collaboration with Jessica Hallonsten, in Kämpinge, Sweden.

*Showcasing
craftsmanship*
—
Skilled craftsmanship
can often be suited to
gardens, and it provides
us with the opportunity
to preserve valuable
heritage as well as to
innovate. Historically,
fences and walls were
made with any materials
that came to hand.
Round-pole fences are
entirely natural and are
made from wood such
as spruce or juniper.
They can be seen across
Scandinavia, but are
mainly found in forested
regions, such as this one
in Dalarna, Sweden.

Defining boundaries
—

Every garden has the
potential to excel, should
we treat it with respect
and work to bring out
the best in it. Looking
at the topography and
vegetation and finding an
immediate relationship
with the landscape
beyond can be a wise
starting point. A sudden
and defined boundary
between constructed
architectural elements
and the natural
environment was the
design impetus for this
terrace by John Robert
Nilsson Arkitektkontor
in Värmdö, Sweden, with
an immense surface of
limestone opening up the
space and connecting
with the panoramic views.

Contrast through detailing
—

Design details can be subtle yet make a huge impact. The detail in this composition by Zetterman Garden Design, in Saltsjö Duvnäs, Sweden, works with mass and void. The water feature is left open underneath the path, making this design feel less restrained. By letting water flow under the edge, a dark shadow is created, providing excitement and contrast within the space.

Analysing the space
—

Opposite: You may have a wealth of inspiration and ideas, but without a plan for implementation it will be hard to achieve a pleasing end result with efficient use of resources. Analysing the space can help you find valuable elements to work with. For example, the trees in this garden by Zetterman Garden Design in Saltsjöbaden, Sweden have been kept, for several reasons: they create spatial awareness, frame views, and provide shelter from winds and neighbouring properties. Moreover they have aesthetic value in themselves – the weeping birch tree in particular is timelessly graceful in a garden where tradition meets current modes of expression.

Flowing space
—

The curves used in this garden by Gullik Gulliksen Landscape Architects, in Lysaker, Norway, bring out its natural flow, making the space inviting to walk through. The size of the curves, which are left open, communicates generosity, while the asymmetry heightens the dynamics. Central to the space is a sweeping lawn, representing the void of the garden, with long and low sections of hedging that gently enclose the perimeter. This hedging is accompanied by taller grass, subtly breaking down the formality.

A relationship with nature
—
One of the objectives
in this garden by
DAP Stockholm in
collaboration with Nod
Combine, in Värmdö,
Sweden, was to preserve
a feeling of nature within
the arranged space.
The deep, dark outdoor
pool captivates, while
the spectrum of natural
colours in the sharp
granite rock connects
with the rampant space
beyond. Gardens can
demonstrate ambition,
yet still show appreciation
for the past by caring
for existing elements.
The granite used here
bears marks dating back
thousands of years, while
its sharp treatment is
starkly contemporary.

Native trees
—

Opposite Pale birch, majestic pine and vigorous spruce are all commonly seen across the region, and the birch is particularly associated with Scandinavia. Due to its growth habit, carrying many small leaves balanced by voids, natural light is filtered through its branches, providing movement and gentle articulation. Swedish botanist Carl von Linné named the birch seen here – *Betula pendula* 'Dalecarlica' – after a small Swedish town, and it is commonly called the Ornäs birch.

Working with the weather
—

We can learn and take inspiration from nature. This outdoor drying rack named the 'Spider Web' by Anders Brøgger for Skagerak is a contemporary expression of Scandinavian resilience. Made out of hardwood teak, which contains a high natural oil content, it is sturdily constructed and able to cope with the harsh weather conditions found in Scandinavia. The wood changes colour over time, eventually taking on a silver-grey patina, making it an aesthetically pleasing outdoor feature as well as providing function.

*Varying sizes of hard
landscape elements*
—
Variation in the size
of hard landscaping
elements gives objects
and entities priority and
hierarchy. When done
with care this can enable
the eye to rest comfortably
in a garden. In this lounge
area by DesignHaver in
Vejle Fjord, Denmark,
large slabs of slate give
weight to the space, while
smaller units balance
the larger shapes without
overpowering. The seating
area, comprising large
light-coloured units, is the
main focus, serving both
as a piece of furniture and
as a sculpture through its
distinctive and solid look.

*Using shape to
give direction*
—
Opposite: Triangles are
powerful shapes that
provide a strong sense
of direction, with the
eye being drawn to the
pointed tip. This garden,
by Haver med Stil, Have-
og Landskabsarkitekt
MAA in Østjylland,
Denmark, implies
stability, using the triangle
shape for the hard
landscaping as well as
in a zigzag pattern in the
low hedging as part of
the soft landscaping. The
seductively deep, dark
colour used repeatedly
for the hedge and in the
brick of the entertaining
area communicates with,
and balances, the façade.

Evocative planting
—
Opposite: Planting is
an essential part of
designing a garden; it
evokes emotions and
provides movement,
colour, and fragrance
in the space. This planting
by Tidens Stauder Design
is situated in sandy soil
in Sealand, Denmark,
and was created with
a naturalistic approach,
connecting to the sky,
sea and sandy dunes
using a combination of
Catananche caerulea,
Sesleria nitida, Atriplex
hortensis purpurea and
Allium 'Purple Sensation'.

*Juxtaposing organic
and geometric shapes*
—
Organic shapes are more
flowing and sweeping
than geometric ones.
The hard landscaping
surrounding this garden
in Roslagen, Sweden,
by Zetterman Garden
Design, carries a wiggly,
curved perimeter,
connecting it to the
countryside beyond,
and contrasting with
the geometric lines of
the swimming pool.
The use of natural paving
stones in a random
pattern further enhances
the informality, also
connecting to the vertical
detailing on the façade
of the house.

Playing with volumes
—
Changing volumes and shapes creates dynamics in a garden. Central to this space in Copenhagen, Denmark by Paradehusets Tegnestue/Paradehuset Landscape Design Studio is the symmetrical sculpture court, partially hidden, which can first be appreciated upon entering the space. It is guarded by tall, slender trees, providing vertical balance. Green globes are placed in an irregular pattern, communicating with the round sculpture in the semi-enclosed space.

Exploiting linear elements
—
Lines make powerful design elements. The generous rectangular walkway in this garden in Asker, Norway by Gullik Gulliksen Landscape Architects give stability to the space, while the dark, polished gabbro stone detailing leads the eye inwards. Visually strong and a refreshing detail, contrasting with the silver-grey slabs, it also echoes the glossy roof of the house. Stretching the walkway on to the smaller paving units, breaking the horizontal base line, makes it more inviting. The soft landscaping in this garden also uses a strong geometric language, with perennials and hedging in strict alignment.

Changing planes
—
Subtle changes of plane, slightly raising or recessing areas, can emphasize elements and create exciting dynamics in a garden, as here in Midwest Jutland, Denmark, in a scheme by Paradehusets Tegnestue/ Paradehuset Landscape Design Studio. Large raised steel-framed beds in this composition frame the planting, and provide interest to the scheme all year round, while the jetty-like bridge interlinks with the paving, clearly marking its position.

Minimalist approach
—
To stay true to one material and change only its direction often proves successful in minimalist schemes. In this garden by Have- og Landskabsarkitektfirmaet AT ApS and Arne Thomsen, in Vejle, Denmark, a generous granite path provides a strong axis, acting as a focal point between the entertaining area and the lawn. Clear alignment of strong rectangles is seen in the granite paving, suggesting intellectual rigour. Taller trees are planted at the perimeter, leaving voids in between, framing the gardens as well as the view beyond.

Entrance considerations
—

Opposite: Front gardens and entrances are spaces seen on a daily basis, and make an instant impression. Detailing, patterns, materials and even the colour of the house can be borrowed and used in the front garden to cohere a scheme. This garden by Østengen & Bergo Landskapsarkitekter in Oslo, Norway makes use of patterns and materials for gates and storage spaces that seamlessly integrate with the house.

*Designing around
a central axis*
—

Developing a design around a strong central axis is useful in organized schemes. An axis is an imaginary line from which the design grows. It can be used to order and align elements. (Things almost, but not entirely, aligned appear worrying to the eye.) In this front garden by Zetterman Garden Design in Saltsjö Duvnäs, Sweden, the design develops from a strong axis running from the entrance. The distribution of repeated hard and soft landscaping elements to both sides of the path, in a rigid grid, stabilizes the design.

Plant list
—

Fargesia murielae
Hedera helix 'Baltica'
Taxus baccata
Carpinus betulus
Festuca gautieri
Calamagrostis
x acutiflora 'Karl Foerster'

Stylish Swedish outdoor living
—

Kämpinge, Sweden
Design by: Johan Sundberg Arkitektur
in collaboration with Jessica Hallonsten
1400m²

Opposite: Timber and decking has strong direction in any garden, providing clear lines in the scheme.

Right: Generous seating areas are situated close to the house for both lounging and dining.

Below: The garden and house resonate as one entity, with large windows facing the garden.

Although the flatlands of Denmark and southern Sweden are mild regions, with a wide selection of suitable plant options, the landscape is exposed to strong winds and the sandy soils often need topping up with mulch to maintain moisture and nutrition levels. Some gardens are hidden in courtyards or surrounded by walls to shelter people and plants from the strong winds. For this family, a couple with three children, spacious entertaining and play areas were a priority, as well as screening off from the nearby street, both in terms of wind and from passers by.

The scale and proportion of an integrated outdoor swimming pool, as well

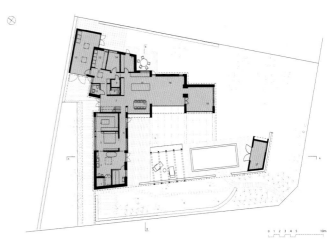

as dining and lounge areas, were the starting points of the layout for the space. There was a need to ensure functionality, utilizing the space to its maximum potential, as well as ensuring that the garden itself remained an attractive feature of the space, with large full-height windows facing on to it.

The swimming pool was the largest entity, measuring 8 × 4 metres, but it was planned so as not to overpower the space. By using a length at least double the width, the rectangular swimming pool was able to align and engage with the nearby tall wall, becoming a precise and architectural focal point. The swimming pool was positioned to be clearly visible, yet situated a comfortable distance away, from the house. This enables the parents to see the children jumping into the water and swimming, yet muffles the sometimes rather loud sound of heavy splashes. At the same time generous space is opened up to entertain close to the house, for those who prefer to stay dry.

The planning of vertical structures in the garden was done with the aim of achieving both privacy and shelter from the sun at relevant times throughout the day, as well as adding visual interest to the space. The solid black pergola structure made from steel and pine is resolute, clearly marking the lounge area. By slightly raising the horizontal plane in this part of the garden, the lounge area is made both more pronounced and more intimate. The wall is integrated into the pergola design by placing one set of black verticals outside the wall. Together, the units allow light and shade to wander through the space throughout the day, creating interesting patterns and shadows.

Furthermore, when walking through a narrow gap between the wall and the storage building, a long, green, lush patch of planting opens up. This courtyard outside the main entertaining area stretches to the perimeter of the plot, enabling further circulation within the garden.

Opposite, above:
An eclectic approach
to furniture choice,
mixing heavy and light
structures, and rustic
and refined, injects life
into the scheme.

Opposite, below: A
generous lawn stretches
out from the entertaining
areas to blend with the
green perimeter around
the garden.

Right: Planting areas
embedded in the hard
landscaping break up the
space, creating natural
walkways and adding a
sense of softness.

Below: One of the beams
makes a perfect frame
for a hammock to laze
in the sun.

SILENT

Playing with the captivating Nordic light

Scandinavians live with natural light that changes dramatically with the seasons. It enchants, casting a spell on people and their gardens alike. The light is so distinctly different throughout the year that it defines us and our lifestyle. Natural light in Scandinavia seems quite different from the light quality further south on the continent. The angle of the sun is much lower approaching the poles, which results in low-intensity light that is perceived as cool and weak.

Just as Scandinavians often talk about the lack of light in the winter months, so we also discuss the weather frequently. Further back in our history, in a time when we lived off the land, the weather was of major importance in ensuring growth and good harvests. Weather and temperature variations, of which we experience many, play a part in how natural light works in a garden and give us spectacular moments – of which the most amazing comes when the Northern Lights (the Aurora Borealis) dance in the night sky.

Glowing grasses
—
Ornamental grasses
such as *Miscanthus*
are exciting to work
with both in daylight
and when artificially
illuminated. Here light
hits the dry plumes at
midday – when the sun
reaches its highest point
above the horizon – in
December, in Stockholm,
Sweden. Light from
behind makes the soft
plumes glow.

Natural light

After the long wait of winter,
Scandinavians crave the light and warmth
of spring, seeking every opportunity to
bask in the sun. Light is also crucial in
order for any living organism to grow. All
plants are developed to absorb light and
make optimal use of it, even plants that
have adapted to thrive in the shade.

Apart from the importance of light to
plants and people, it allows for creativity
within a design scheme. To make
maximum use of the light in a garden,
however, it is important to understand
the garden's orientation, and how the sun
moves through the space. In large gardens,
which provide enough space for several
seating and entertaining areas, these
areas might face the sun at different times
throughout the day, and conversely this
means that there will be an alternative
option to sit in a shady spot if that
is desired.

Making a space lighter or darker

All materials have a surface texture, or
a finish, and when light strikes a surface
it can be absorbed or reflected. To what
degree this happens depends on the finish
of the surface. A polished stone or a glossy
leaf will make light bounce off its surface.
This can be helpful in darker areas of a
garden where more light is desired, but
could be undesirable in direct sunshine,
where the light may become too strong.
Some plants with glossy foliage have the
potential to brighten a shady situation,
such as *Asarum europaeum* or *Mahonia*.
Other plants may not be glossy but have
bright foliage, such as the variegated
varieties *Brunnera macrophylla* 'Dawson's
White' and *Hosta fortunei* 'Patriot',
which boosts light through its colour in
a dark corner.

Meanwhile a matt finish absorbs light,
making a surface look opaque and the
foliage of plants more diffuse. Examples
of plants with matt and light-absorbing

foliage are *Artemisia, Alchemilla* and *Cerastium*.

Colour and surface texture together determine the qualities of a surface. A very dark colour absorbs a lot of heat and may be uncomfortable to walk across on hot summer days. A too-bright paving stone does not get hot, but might reflect too much light and be blinding in direct sunlight; it would be better suited to a darker area of the garden.

The local area can provide a guide to the colours and textures appropriate to a particular garden. Hard landscaping in Scandinavia, from volcanic regions in Iceland to the majestic mountains of Norway, and from barren cliffs in the archipelagos of Finland and Sweden to the sandy soils of Denmark contain a range of mid-grey, neutral tones, with a matt or semi-matt finish, appearing somewhat diffuse or toned down. This is why a very prominent stone such as white marble doesn't sit well in a Scandinavian garden.

Light and shadow

Open surfaces, especially those arranged on one level, can appear flat. Sometimes this works well in the context of a design. At other times, adding structures can give more of a sense of intimacy in a space. They can provide privacy and also create depth, variation and excitement with shadows.

Compared to artificial light that uses electricity, we cannot adjust natural light. However, we can play with it, with the result being interesting patterns, and sometimes quite theatrical shows put on by light hitting a structure. Vertical structures, for example, can enable static or dynamic shadows. Semi-open structures such as a pergolas can be functionally pleasing, with sunbeams partially penetrating, toning down the light intensity in an over-exposed area, as well as lending visual interest to a seating area. By adding static verticals such as pergolas, trellises and other screening into the scheme, light and

shadow take on a new relationship and give the garden another dimension. These cast shadows seem static, just like the structure, but in fact change throughout the day and season with the movement of the sun: its direction and intensity, and the length of daylight. Shadows may be stretched and diffuse, sometimes to the point of surreality, especially in winter when the sun is low and shadows become excessive in length.

Structures that move in the garden, such as the foliage of trees and plants, create more dynamic shadows. When the midsummer sun gets too much, dappled shade from a tree can provide the perfect escape. Lying down on the ground or in a hammock, with the overhead peaceful

Shadow contouring
—
A gentle void provides a sense of lightness in this garden by DesignHaver in Vedbæk, Denmark, enabling a cast shadow to act as a fine detail and effectively providing contouring in the design. The two solid structures – the patio floor and the stone edge – enjoy a spatial relationship as two separate entities that give the area a certain grace and elegance.

view of the sky filtered through birch foliage is familiar to many Scandinavians. The more movement that can be found in the soft landscaping, the more energy will be reflected in the shadows cast, imbuing the garden with drama and life. Tall and light perennials with pronounced flower heads, for example *Anemone × hybrida* 'Honorine Jobert' and *Papaver orientale*, and ornamental grasses with similar body, such as *Miscanthus* and *Calamagrostis*, provide pronounced shadows with a distinctive shape and splendour.

Shadows are especially interesting as they are temporary, coming and going seemingly at will and sometimes making comic appearances in the far north, often providing more interest than the object itself. With the sun at a low angle, especially in the mornings and evenings, shadows don't only showcase the element itself, but also reveal fine detailing such as a surface texture, or a slightly recessed joint in a paved area.

Light constantly changes a garden

The constantly changing natural light has a startling effect on the colours in a garden. On a sunny summer's day in Scandinavia, light floods a space more or less around the clock. The energy from the sun seems to be transmitted to everything living and gardens are usually full of activity, with diffuse sounds and pleasant smells. We open up our houses, throw parties, eat, entertain, chat and laugh endlessly during the lively, extended evenings. Colours are at their most intense around midday, when the light appears white. Any water close by, or open space in a garden where sunbeams hit, bounces light to the surrounding areas, resulting in even brighter spaces.

Later in the season, there is an array of pastels in the sky, from warm coral pinks, to purples and blues, which become especially pronounced during twilight. With lower temperatures and moisture in the air, a garden can seem mystical, with structures vaguely glimpsed and the landscape almost seeming to breathe. Late summer mornings bring breathtakingly beautiful scenes, with light breaking through the fog as it evaporates with the rising temperature. Sunrise brings an incredible glow to the garden for a fleeting moment as, like shining crystals, every drop of water clinging to the plants refracts the first rays.

Before the first snowfall, it is particularly noticeable how important light is in the north – the approaching lack of it is daunting. Long winters and days with very few hours of daylight have resulted in Scandinavians embracing bright and light in all their manifestations. What natural light is available seems especially tranquil and delightful in winter, filled with subtle colours, and giving the garden a dazzling touch – but only for a few hours. Gardens are quiet, saving their energy just as people do at this time of year, and snow gives the landscape a soft and soothing air. Sometimes the moon and the Northern Lights together provide a spectacular light. But the focus is then on artificial lighting during the darkest winter months, to give both gardens and people comfort.

A sense of depth
—
Light and shadow give depth to a garden, allowing us to see texture, dimension and perspective more clearly. When designing gardens it is tempting to think primarily of light; to aim for a bright garden or an illuminated space. Shadows, however, are what give a garden character and enable an understanding of the space, as in this garden by Zetterman Garden Design in Saltsjöbaden, Stockholm.

Designing with light

As much as the natural light can be enchanting and vivid, the darkness in Scandinavia can be overwhelming. With the natural light so pronounced around midsummer in Scandinavia, additional light at this time of year is redundant. White snow falling is always uplifting during the deepest darkness of winter, but artificial lighting to supplement the natural light is still much needed at times. With the growing efficiency of stable LEDs (light-emitting diodes) in recent years, the interest in illuminating gardens has also risen, and today outdoor lighting is an essential part of many Scandinavian gardens.

The benefit of using artificial lighting is that we can control it and decide on the position of the source, as well as when and to what degree an area should be illuminated. Planning for lighting is as essential as planning any other part of a garden, and lights can be incorporated in many different ways. Exterior lighting has two distinct purposes. First, it should be functional and provide safety in a garden. Second, it should be aesthetically pleasing and create harmony in the space. Just like natural light, artificial lighting can be used to create visual effects, to appear to enlarge objects, make water seem magical in the evenings and cast interesting shadows on feature walls.

The importance of darkness

When planning for lighting fixtures in a garden there is one single element, without which our endeavours would be meaningless: darkness. Without darkness we would not be able to see the light. With too many lighting fixtures, darkness is eliminated and a garden appears chaotic and confused; the eye can find nowhere to rest. The key to a successful lighting composition is to leave some areas unlit. Balancing illuminated spaces with darkness creates dynamic contrast, and the space will resonate with tranquil unity. Artificial lighting is a powerful tool, and gives a sharper contrast and depth to a space than natural shadows and light. We can enhance dimensions, highlight sculptures or simply make an object much more prominent. A backlit wall panel or a lit trellis set away from a wall can make a unique feature in the evening.

Finely tuned lighting
—
Successful illumination in a garden often comes as a result of careful fine tuning, paying attention to the intensity, direction and spread of light. Two objects are highlighted in this garden in Värmdö, Sweden by Zetterman Garden Design: a corten steel fire pit, acting as a sculpture when not in use, and a *Magnolia stellata*. Darkness enables the objects to communicate and be highlighted, leaving a dark void between the entities.

Be selective with lighting

When planning for a successful lighting scheme in a garden, consider placing lights on different levels in the space, for example recessed in the ground, at eye-level and some that either reach or come from higher up. This will give variation in intensity and interest, and heighten the sense of space. This is also achieved by placing lights in different parts of the garden, not only close to the house. Moreover, it is wise to be practical with light and place sources where they are most useful: a driveway, for instance, needs a light positioned high enough in a region with potentially heavy snowfall. Being selective in the range of light fittings and using the same light fitting repeatedly unifies a space. Illumination is not successfully achieved just by the choice of light fittings and their position, but is also the result of fine tuning the details to achieve the effect and function desired. It is important that the light is strong enough to reach where it is meant to reach, but equally that it is not too strong, bouncing off too much or reaching too far. The spread should be just sufficient, or it may be perceived as too sharp or too diffuse. The colour of outdoor lighting is subjective and there are no rules as to what works best, but in general a slightly warm light is appreciated; it doesn't look sterile and cold when aesthetics are the prime concern, while a neutral white light is preferred when function is the focus.

Direct and indirect light

Lighting can be direct or indirect, and combining direct and indirect lighting provides variation in a design. A direct light, often pointing down, is light that is directly pointing at a surface. This light is often perceived as straightforward and hard, and is often used for driveways, entrances and parking spaces. An indirect light, often pointing up, comes from fixtures which give direction to light and

Degree of illumination
—
How much illumination is appropriate in a garden can be discussed in terms of light pollution, so as not to disturb areas around the given space. Lighting may also be influenced by personal preferences; some people prefer darker gardens, while others like to see them lit up. Depending on where the garden is situated, it may require a particular level of lighting. An open garden next to a wide landscape naturally lets more ambient light into the space, like this garden next to a bay in Saltsjöbaden, Stockholm by Zetterman Garden Design.

can bounce off something else in the garden. This might be a wall, a tree or a sculpture, for example. Indirect lighting is ideal for creating atmosphere in a garden. Sometimes it is intended to be decorative and functional at the same time – for instance, sufficient lighting in a hedge close to an access will make the hedge glow, but will spread light on to the path as well.

Lighting can be incorporated into both soft and hard landscaping structures in a garden. A wall can be lit to accentuate fine surface textures that are otherwise not as pronounced in daylight. Arches and overhead structures can be framed with shapes that make them look rather dramatic at night compared with their appearance in natural daylight. Trees are portrayed as very sculptural when indirectly lit, displaying vigorous bare branches as well as decorative bark. Tall pine trees look even more majestic when uplit, and trees such as *Betulas*, *Prunus serrula*, *Acer griseum* and *Acer pensylvanicum* deserve to display their incredible bark, both with and without foliage. Interesting seed heads can look spectacular when backlit. Hydrangeas, for instance, keep their flower heads through autumn and winter.

Scandinavians have an affinity with water, with the sea bordering all countries, and plenty of lakes. Outdoor bathing and swimming are common and are even undertaken in winter by the brave, whether in a hot spring in Iceland, a lake (and sauna to follow) in Finland, off the cliffs on the Swedish west coast, or by a sandy beach in Denmark. Water features in gardens vary in type and size. In general, more subtle water elements can be found – a small birdbath, a calm water feature, a swimming pool or sometimes a pond – elements that make only rather gentle movements and sounds. Incorporating light into water features such as a swimming pool instantly brings out fascinating movement and depth, and is useful in terms of safety aspects for

people and animals, as well as serving a decorative purpose in the evenings. Lighting and calm waters combined in darkness can give a theatrical, captivating effect. Large expanses of water such as a swimming pool also provide light and dancing reflections to animate the area nearby.

Environmental aspects

Artificial light is attractive but can become too much if used to excess. Although illuminating gardens is of much practical use, you should also be aware of environmental aspects when designing with light, and plan its use wisely. Cost-effective, widely accessible outdoor lighting doesn't have to mean using excessive amounts. Allowing for areas of darkness will balance a composition as well as letting our sensitive ecosystem thrive as necessary. Wildlife and birds, as well as various nocturnal species, may be disturbed by areas of intense lighting. It is wise to concentrate light on areas where most time is spent in the garden. If there are parts of a garden very close to or bordering on the natural landscape, try leaving these unlit.

Cities and people are also affected by too much artificial light. Plan light to be directional within the garden rather than intensely glowing beyond the garden. Make use of automated units, timers and devices such as remote lighting switches for greater efficiency. Consider planning light on several circuits, to enable detailed programming and control of the lighting in a garden. Today's advanced systems give complete control over how you wish to steer the lights, and when you wish to have them switched on or off. You don't want the artificial light to eclipse more naturally mesmerizing moments in the garden, when the full moon and stars animate the space.

*Enhancing the character
of weak light*
—
The light at noon is the
most balanced light,
appearing nearly white,
while light in the early
morning or afternoon
can provide an array
of colour variations.
Natural light changes
frequently, and so gardens
also constantly change
in their colours, often
appearing extremely
subtle in the characteristic
low light in Scandinavia.
This garden by Zetterman
Garden Design, situated
close to a bay in
Värmdö, Stockholm, is
enchantingly calm on a
still day dominated by
a beautiful, weak light.

The influence of the sea
—
Seaside gardens are innately bright, made lighter by the reflections off the water close by. By placing a water feature or a swimming pool in a seaside garden, the space naturally connects with the surroundings, and further light is spread to the garden. This infinity pool, in a design by Jarmund/Vigsnæs AS Arkitekter MNAL in Vestfold, Norway, overlooks the open sea. A glass fence forms the outer perimeter of the pool, making the most of the view, while also protecting against the wind. Durable kebony wood is used for the terrace, weathering with grace in the strong winds and damp, salty air.

This long, symmetrical, shallow mirror pool in a scheme by Paradehusets Tegnestue/Paradehuset Landscape Design Studio in Mid Jutland, Denmark is interrupted by a copper freestanding espalier screen, echoing the precise architectural lines elsewhere in the design. The screens reflect in the mirror pool while also creating a semi-transparent background, breaking, but not closing off the view of the surrounding hills.

Shadows from above
—

Opposite: Shadows can be created by various lattices and meshes in overhead structures and screening. They can distinctively animate a space, casting shadows through the voids, and distorting or stretching patterns. This principle is shown at work in this garden by Johan Sundberg Arkitektur in Höllviken, Sweden, where the screening also can be moved along the decking and positioned at will.

Semi-transparent structures
—

Structures create excitement when they interact with natural light. Using semi-transparent glass panels in front of objects, especially moving entities, can create theatrical visual interest in a garden. The static panel in this garden by Gullik Gulliksen Landscape Architects in Drøbak, Norway makes use of slender ornamental grasses behind the screen, with plants displaying only their freely moving silhouettes.

Light for plants to thrive
—
Armeria maritima, commonly known as thrift, can be found in the wild in all parts of Scandinavia, and is also often used as a plant in gardens. If you take a stroll along any sandy beach or cliff you may be greeted with a sea of these purple flower heads. Light is crucial for any plant to grow, and it is important to know how much light a plant requires for it to thrive and bloom. A plant that is viewed as a spring plant in southern Scandinavia may flower much later in the season in northern regions. These small, pale, globe-shaped clusters of flowers and slender stalks in Ölmanäs, Sweden, seem as fragile as the Scandinavian light itself on a late summer evening.

*Light for spatial
awareness*
—
Light can gently frame
entertaining areas and
create spatial awareness.
Staying true to the use
of cedar wood throughout
this terrace by Minarc
in Kiðjaberg, Iceland,
with simple changes
in structure and lines,
the benches are made
sculptural as well as
functional. Subtle
floodlighting under the
benches gently frames,
without imposing upon
the house lighting scheme
or the surrounding
natural environment.

Subtle articulation of linear elements
—
Outdoor lights can show vigour and be subtle at the same time, which is shown well in this garden in Stockholm, Sweden by DAP Stockholm in collaboration with Nod Combine. By placing a recessed narrow floodlight close to the significant line between the arranged space and the rampant garden in this scheme, authority is given to the linear shape at the same time as it comfortably illuminates the granite rock.

Social lighting
—
Outdoor lighting can increase the time we spend outside socializing. Placing lighting around lounge and entertainment areas makes them more inviting to use. In this garden by DesignHaver in Jutland, Denmark, the comfortable glow accentuates both the architectural shape of the seating unit and the texture of the standing boulders behind. Temporary light, candles, fires and the reflection and light from the moon will make the evening even more memorable.

Placing light at different
heights in a garden, with
some sources near to the
ground while others aim
higher, as well as ensuring
distribution in various
places, creates a spatial
effect in a garden in the
evenings. This young
Acer griseum in a space
by Zetterman Garden
Design in Saltsjöbaden,
Sweden is gently lit up
with just the right degree
of illumination.

*Design elements
intensified*
—
The combination of
functionality and visual
interest is exciting to
explore when working
with light in gardens.
Already defined shapes
are intensified in this
front garden by Zetterman
Garden Design in
Saltsjöbaden, Sweden,
seen here at night. The
walking bridge marks an
undisturbed and powerful
line in the space, while
the depth and outline of
the countersunk circular
element are pronounced,
making a secret pit.

59

Outdoor fireplaces
—

Opposite: Incorporating fireplaces into a garden can produce magical moments. This scheme in Southern Funen, Denmark, by DesignHaver (Olymp fireplace by Tor Haddeland) incorporates several fireplaces for optimal use, seen from different angles of the garden. The upper fire, integrated with the house, guards the amphi-terrace, while the lower fireplace becomes a focal point incorporated into the lounge area, where flames dance through a layer of marine gravel.

Manipulating lighting effects
—

Position and direction are important aspects when designing with light. The natural light on this foliage in Fredrikstad, Norway demonstrates how differently things can appear depending on where the light hits. The leaf in the middle, glowing and showing all its veins, is an example of light coming from behind and underneath. Meanwhile the bottom leaf shows how light falls on the top of the surface, not enhancing the colour or the leaf structure.

Highlighting features
—

Opposite: Light can make objects appear more prominent. An ornamental tree may provide a pleasant surprise; the branching structure of smaller, multi-stemmed trees such as *Cornus mas* and *Amelanchier lamarckii* may be intensified using a ground-mounted fixture. Trees standing close to a wall can be silhouetted with the wall as a bright backdrop. The character of this *Crataegus monogyna* in a design by DesignHaver in Aalborg, Denmark, is pronounced by uplighting the tree and concentrating light on the stem and canopy.

Framing a narrow space
—

On a late October evening in Stockholm, Sweden, the sky is lit with an array of pastels. Natural light spreads freely on to this rather narrow, urban roof terrace by Zetterman Garden Design, which is situated high up with panoramic views. Lighting has been used as an important design tool for this terrace, as it maximizes and opens up the narrow space. It frames pergola structures, enhances planting and is used indirectly under wooden benches. Wall-mounted lights spread a soft, wide-angled glow.

Tranquil daylight in a Scandinavian summer garden adds another dimension to this space in Aalborg, Denmark, designed by DesignHaver and Tor Haddeland. It seems to calm surfaces, casting long and diffuse shadows across the garden. A water feature in this garden enhances the sense of quiet in the space, and incorporates a floating fireplace for visual interest by day or night. The black on the inside surface of a low water feature gives an illusion of depth to the water.

House lighting
—
Lighting outside houses should provide safety and appear pleasant – as natural as possible, and not penetrating. When planning for lights in a garden consider how much light the house itself provides, both from the interior, through windows, and on the exterior façade. This house entrance in Kämpinge, Sweden, designed by Johan Sundberg Arkitektur, uses downlighting that leads the eye to the entrance as well as uplighting on a nearby tree, which becomes a sculptural element in the evening.

Lighting and water
—
Combining artificial light and water can prove very effective at night, with distinct reflections and shadows on the surface of still water. In this atrium garden in Sandefjord, Norway by Gullik Gulliksen Landscape Architects, the water feature and the illuminated sculptural plants form an artistic effect and give a warm glow to the garden at night.

Lighting as sculpture
—

Garden lights can act as sculptural elements in themselves. With many parts of Scandinavia experiencing harsh winters, typical garden focal points such as clay pots must often be brought inside if they are not designed to withstand extreme cold. This bollard by Zetterman Garden Design in a garden in Saltsjö Duvnäs, Stockholm passes for a sculpture in the space as much as it functions as a light.

Clear guidance
—

Opposite: Function is an important aspect when working with lights in a garden to ensure safety. Here LED light floods beneath the stairs in this entrance by DesignHaver in Vedbæk, Denmark, clearly marking each step. The circular light fittings, repeatedly and evenly recessed in the granite paving, shed light onto the wall, leading the way and making the path more welcoming. The dots contrast with the linear shapes and squares in the space, forming a refreshing design detail along the pathway.

Expression and safety
—

Function marries with aesthetics through the lighting composition in this garden. By using gentle curves this access road in a scheme by Gullik Gulliksen Landscape Architects in Lysaker, Norway leads straight to the entrance – but with added excitement. Using a strong solid line to one side enhances the design but also forms a platform to incorporate sculptural bollards. By slightly raising the surface and with the bollards pointing towards the driveway the design expression also gives guidance, especially in darkness and in winter, when the bollards will remain visible even in deep snow.

Lighting to animate a night-time space in Denmark

—

Vedbæk, Denmark
Design by: DesignHaver
890m²

A garden that is functional and attractive in daylight may lose both qualities in the dark, especially during the winter months in Scandinavia, when the darkness can be penetrating. In a garden that is limited in size, a strict focus on the main objective and perhaps the use of multifunctional modules can be an efficient way of maximizing the space, both visually and functionally. A tactic that works well in narrow spaces is to use lights as a design element in themselves.

The wish list for this family garden, situated north of Copenhagen, was originally quite long, and it was important to establish what was most important at the outset. Eventually the brief was reduced to the following: an inviting entrance, space for a double garage, a lounge area and an outdoor dining area. In the scheme lighting becomes a kind of embroidery on the design at night.

This garden has been designed by using two sets of lines: one parallel to the house, the other set at a slight angle. Combining these two geometries, the space breaks up into separate units, with each area having a dedicated function. Subtle changes in levels were planned for

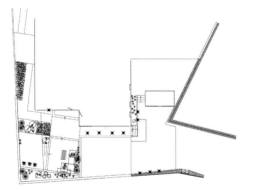

practical reasons, but also to give gentle articulation and framing. To maximize space, the rear wall of the garage is utilized as a backdrop to the lounge area. This formed a countersunk area of garden; a peaceful oasis in the corner, including topiary acting as sculptures in the space, well suited to illumination. Lighting enables prolonged use of the garden in the summer evenings in Denmark, and provides embellishment when the garden is viewed from the house.

Lighting is situated throughout the garden, with several indirect sources hidden under the rim of the steps, for visual effect and to show the change of level. Solid seating units are also illuminated from underneath, providing a comfortable light that does not spread uncontrolled across the garden or into neighbouring gardens. Lighting in this small garden transforms it into a new, inspiring place, highlighting topiary and strongly architectural plants.

Top: The garden takes on a new character in the evening, when dark voids are encouraged to complement illuminated entities.

Above: Large glass elevations let natural light into the house as well as allowing generous views of the garden.

Opposite: Topiary that is sculptural even in daylight is amplified and clearly defined by lighting at night, enhancing the characteristics of its branches and foliage for a theatrical effect.

FRAGILE

Principles of selecting and growing plants

When inheriting a garden, it might not be obvious at first what plants are in the space – a closer look could reveal old and perhaps even rare treasures. Traditionally in Scandinavia, plants were not chosen for their architectural and ornamental interest as they are today. The focus in the past was on growing edible plants, with gardens containing fruit trees – mainly apples – vegetables and sometimes herbs.

Today, however, gardens are created that often contain both edible and ornamental plants. The scope for creating artistic and design-centric planting schemes is greater than ever with the wide range of plants available at nurseries. With so much choice we have the potential for great expression, and for gardens to look attractive all year round.

Designing with plants

Planting is often viewed as one of the more exciting aspects of the planning process. Aside from its aesthetic value, soft landscaping protects people and wildlife alike. Green spaces produce the oxygen that we breathe and help with garden drainage. Plants also provide shelter and food to wildlife, which by extension helps with our own survival.

However, it is easy to become overwhelmed by the planting options available. Although there are many plants that don't suit the Scandinavian climate, you may be surprised at the vast selection that do thrive in the region. What limitations there are, though, might be viewed positively, as they can enhance creativity; you might find new uses for a particular plant within a design. For instance ornamental grasses, which provide interest in winter, can work as a substitute for evergreen plants, which are less viable in the far north. Unlike many other countries, Scandinavia experiences very distinct seasonal variations, enjoying for example incredibly colourful autumnal spectra. As in any other country, though, our palette of plants is part of our regional identity, and it is a much greater pleasure to wear this identity with pride and relish our heritage, rather than be disappointed at the plants we can't grow such as tree ferns, *Heliconia* and *Protea*.

With solid knowledge of plants and their requirements, use of design principles and an artistic eye you are bound to succeed with a planting composition. Plants can imbue a space with very specific feelings, so be firm in knowing what you want to communicate, and follow your plan. The actual composition is subjective and your individual choice of plants and colour – what you think suits the scheme – will give long-lasting pleasure. Plan the soft landscaping primarily with shapes and

Formal and informal lines
—
This garden in Jutland, Denmark by Kjeld Slot of Haver & Landskaber uses strong lines in a powerful zigzag pattern formed by the dark green foliage of the *Ligustrum vulgare* hedging. As elegant detailing, the same zigzag pattern appears in the long, narrow path running down the garden. Washed-out white and silvery perennials and grasses, contrasting with the formality with their sweeping gestures, accentuate the shape of the hedge and seem to come forward against the darker backdrop, while *Pyrus salicifolia* 'Pendula' provides vertical interest.

Shrubs provide interest
—
Shrubs can provide high impact in a garden without too much work, in a border or planted as a mass or a specimen. *Cotinus*, *Cornus*, rhododendrons, hydrangeas, viburnums and conifers all work well in this role, forming a sturdy backbone to a garden. Many shrubs provide interest through foliage, branches and the shapes they make, while others keep their flowers for a long period, such as the ample dusky pink flower heads of this *Hydrangea macrophylla*, seen in autumn in Stockholm, Sweden.

structures in mind to ensure year round interest. Planting schemes can be created in several ways, from using clusters of the same plant in larger blocks to provide a massing effect, to planning for each plant to appear individually in a repeating grid, resulting in a more random-looking and loose creation.

Structure and shape

Each plant has unique qualities, which become evident when it is used in the right way. A plant that you may think less of on its own can look stunning when combined with others. In a successful planting scheme plants interact and have relationships; they create patterns, variation, balance and rhythm – and they complement each other. This is achieved through variation of different kinds – size, shape, texture and colour. Essentially, apart from interesting bark, plants have two main parts that should be considered in a design scheme: the form of the leaves and the form of the flower. Plants can for example have round or oval leaves, or they can be linear. *Ligularia dentata* 'Desdemona' is a plant with round leaves, *Salvia officinalis purpurascens* shows example of oval leaves, while irises have upright and linear foliage. By combining different-shaped foliage, the border becomes more dynamic. Likewise, the head of a flower has different shapes: buttons such as *Scabiosa*, globes like *Echinops bannaticus*, spires like *Veronicastrum virginicum* 'Apollo' or plumes like *Astilbe*. Every plant that you select should have a purpose in the scheme and communicate with those around; it may also have additional qualities such as a seasonal interest, or be attractive to insect life. With a thorough scheme, interest in the soft landscaping should be found every season, sometimes with an ever-changing look.

A Scandinavian garden does not necessarily contain lots of evergreen plants, but often relies on the framework of deciduous plants, retaining interesting structures in winter. A multi-stemmed tree; bright, shiny rosehips spreading out over branches of a naked rose – also a delight for birds; or torch-like plumes in the top of a bare *Rhus* all add to a winter garden. Winter gardens have very little movement, but energy can still be found in some perennials and ornamental grasses with dead seed heads; *Rudbeckia*, *Eryngium*, *Phlomis*, *Pennisetum* and *Miscanthus* for example, which entirely keep their form and move in the wind.

Pattern, repetition and rhythm

In successful planting schemes there is an engaging hook – something that demands attention, making you want to participate in the space. It may be a colour, movement or scent, but most likely it is the overall feeling of many elements combined, which is sometimes hard to describe. The underlying concept, making us feel familiar and comfortable, is to use repetition in planting, meaning a plant regularly recurs in the scheme. By doing this on several occasions, we create a pattern; the combination of using different plants, with contrasting foliage, colours, shape, size and texture. This is what grabs the attention. With a systematic change between patterns and repetition a border acquires rhythm, providing flow, motion and movement to a planting.

Foliage

Foliage is the body of all soft landscaping, comprising plants, sedum roofs, meadows and lawns. It provides the bulk in any planting scheme and should always be planned with great care, as it normally lasts much longer than flower heads, which bloom for a limited time.

The amount of variation in the foliage that is suited to a composition depends on the precise expression you have in mind for the space. For a seaside garden you might want your planting to look airy and light, with numerous examples of fine foliage and a few pronounced leaves only at the base, providing a solid lower structure to the planting. In a formal planting scheme you might want to work with foliage with little movement and a limited selection of plants to clearly frame the hard landscaping and mark every corner and shape.

Options to be creative with foliage are endless and, again, subjective – depending on what you want to communicate. How shapes, colour and texture resonate with the hard landscaping should be considered. Combining a grey stone with silvery or grey-green foliage provides little divergence within the overall scheme, resulting in an almost monochrome, rather sedate and calm expression – while using dark green, red or lime green foliage will result in a strong contrast to a grey paving stone, where each material looks clear and sharp. For further variation, a scheme can also include plants with variegated leaves containing both green and non-green parts, commonly whites and yellows.

Creativity with shrubs and grasses

Structures in a garden can be formed of both hard and soft landscaping elements. Hard landscaping is the horizontal and vertical planes of materials such as wood and stone, while soft landscaping refers to living structures, plants, hedges and trees.

Balanced colour and shapes
—
This planting in Jutland, Denmark by Kjeld Slot of Haver & Landskaber shows a body of foliage balanced through colour and shapes. The vertical *Iris variegata* is central to the scheme, changing the rhythm with its sharp and upright foliage. It is accompanied in colour by the *Carex elata aurea* just behind. Although both are upright, the slender grass contrasts with the thickness characterized by the iris. Colour also connects with the foliage of *Ligustrum ovalifolium* 'Aureum' in the background.

An efficient way of balancing the formal and informal, when working with soft structures only, is to add sections of tall grasses and clipped hedges into the scheme. A hedge suitable for clipping and shaping, such as *Carpinus betulus*, *Fagus sylvatica* 'Atropurpurea' or *Ligustrum* gives the garden strong geometry while grasses provide delicacy, being both upright and sturdy. A clipped hedge can – like a wall or screening – act as a backdrop to perennial borders, and hedges alone can be used within a garden to break up the space, while tall grasses provide semi-solid vertical height.

Using naturally strong plants

Just as with hard landscaping, the plants that we choose are meant to stay, and look healthy, in the garden for years to come. Having a sensible approach to the choices of plants for the scheme and selecting plants that naturally thrive where they will be planted is fundamental to

success. Knowledge of the local climate, exposure and soil provides a good starting point, as does observing the plants that thrive in the surrounding landscape. Nurseries and garden centres provide a huge range of plants, including certified locally grown plants that are worth considering in the planting scheme. These plants have qualities such as extra-hardiness, are strongly resistant to diseases and have been tested in several places and are used to the climate conditions, so they should require less maintenance. Schemes in which plants look at their best will reward you in years to come, while unnatural planting and habitats with modified soils are most likely to fail and look out of place.

Wildlife meadows

As much as we are bothered by the hordes of mosquitoes and wasps in summer in Scandinavia, wildlife is part of a garden and all creatures should be looked after, even loved. Wildlife is vital to our ecosystems and we should encourage more of small creatures in our gardens, by considering their needs within the design scheme. Insects, bees and butterflies survive on the nectar of flowers and plants, which is why variation in planting is essential, designed to attract different species throughout the seasons.

When driving through the landscape in Scandinavia around midsummer, you will see the verges provide true works of art with stunning compositions of wild flowers, created by nature itself: magenta-pink *Chamerion angustifolium*, delicate *Campanula rotundifolia*, subtle *Geum rivale*, and sunkissed *Ranunculus acris*.

Dedicating an area of meadow is worth considering for planned gardens as well. It can look enchantingly attractive, blending with the surrounding landscape and providing protection and a habitat for insects. Meadows are ideal for open and exposed areas and are also perfect for problematic areas, such as steep slopes or infertile soil, or as a naturalistic alternative

Use of variegated foliage
—
Variegated foliage is valuable when many colour variations are desired, and may compensate for a lack of coloured blooms, such as in this garden by Tidens Stauder Design in Sealand, Denmark. Foliage can be striped or bordered with a colour, and may be lighter or darker than the rest of the plant. Hosta is appreciated for its foliage colour variations, ranging from white to greys and blues, to lime green and yellow. *Hosta fortunei* 'Patriot' has white margins that brighten a shady corner.

to a lawn, or parts of a lawn. They typically consist of a combination of wild flowers, herbs and grasses, with plants suited to the natural habitat, whether wetland areas, dry conditions or shade. Some common meadow plants include *Centaurea jacea*, *Cynosurus cristatus*, *Galium verum*, *Knautia arvensis*, *Saxifraga granulata*, *Helictotrichon pubescens*, *Campanula persicifolia* and *Lotus corniculatus*. As meadows self-seed, they need to be left until the autumn before being cut. From an aesthetic point of view they are interesting as they vary from year to year, with some species prominent one year and others appearing the next. Wildlife meadows look very free and unconstrained, with species appearing scattered, random and loose, and with most plants humble and yet fine in both their foliage and flowers, providing an excellent contrast to the more constrained elements in a garden.

Trees

Trees, the roof to any garden, are truly majestic, valuable plants, and should be cared for accordingly. Trees have many positive attributes: they break strong winds, they are a safe place for birds to nest, they protect parts of the garden from over-exposure, and they are so-called 'green lungs' for cities. Deep forests in Scandinavia contain a lot of spruce, while pine forests dominate on dry and sandy soils. Birch trees grow in most parts from the very north to the south, while beech trees thrive only in the southern regions. Scandinavians have, through history and still today, a great interest in fruit trees – as long as the harvest doesn't become an unbearable burden with fruits falling and covering the entire garden floor! Pears, plums and cherries are all common, but apple is the signature tree, and all can be found in both old and new gardens.

The question is often whether to keep existing trees in a garden, and if so, which ones. Look at trees carefully, investigate how healthy they are, and consider how they can be incorporated into a design as they might be of huge value, for privacy, shade and also in terms of the composition. The character of a mature tree and its impressive canopy is hard to replace – it takes time. A mature tree planted in the right location will give your new garden an abundance of character and make the space feel instantly genuine.

When planning a garden to include new trees, it is essential to consider their size, height and spread to ensure they suit the area. Trees that grow too vigorously or too tall can drown a small garden. Once a tree is in the ground it is there to stay for decades to come. Ornamental trees such as *Syringa vulgaris* 'Michel Buchner', *Acer palmatum* 'Osakazuki' and *Amelanchier lamarckii* are perfect for a smaller garden, while columnar, fastigiated trees might be considered as tall verticals in narrow spaces – think of *Sambucus nigra*, 'Black Tower' and *Carpinus betulus* 'Frans Fontaine'.

Expression of vigour
—
Ovate and cone-shaped plants, and narrow, upright conifers give a strong visual direction in a garden through their pointed appearance. In the same way our beloved *Syringa* flowers express vigour, appreciated for their scent and early blooms in summer. *Hydrangea paniculata* 'Limelight' and *Hydrangea paniculata* 'Grandiflora' give a similar effect, and the rounded growth habit makes them ideal to mix with slender ornamental grasses to provide contrast, as in this garden by Zetterman Garden Design in Saltsjö Duvnäs, Sweden.

Ornamental grasses

Ornamental grasses are among the most versatile plants in Scandinavia and there are many reasons to use them. Grasses exude simplicity – in their body, their plumes and their colour – and seem somehow close to our roots. The lightness they possess connects us to nature. Some grasses look as novel in summer as they do in winter, maintaining the upright vitality and vertical interest in the garden from early spring and through winter, such as *Molinia caerulea* 'Variegata', *Calamagrostis × acutiflora* 'Overdam' and *Deschampsia cespitosa*. Many grasses are able to withstand harsh conditions, and can cope with winds and droughts as well as the cold. Grasses can be useful as the backbone and structure in a planting scheme, also providing support to other plants, and they suit both urban environments and gardens in rural areas. In cities, gardens may contain a lot of hard landscaping, and grasses provide contrast, looking light and relaxed, while also looking natural in a garden in the country, connecting to the surrounding landscape, which probably also contains grasses.

Shrubs

Shrubs and hedges – rather dense with varying heights – are often useful when we wish to achieve a sense of intimacy, and they can frame or break up spaces. Shrubs can be used in numerous places in a garden, embedded in borders, planted as specimens or providing focal points. Large specimen shrubs can look stunning and act as multi-stemmed sculptures in gardens when they are given the space required, such as *Rosa pimpinellifolia* 'Plena', commonly seen in Finland, *Halesia tetraptera* or *Magnolia sieboldii*. Shrubs can be planted in the form of a shrubbery for a mass effect, where rhododendrons work well, or they can mark the perimeter of a garden.

Always remember to plan for both function and aesthetics. As with any plant, a shrub will look at its best when given the space required for its mature growth. Shrubs not suited to a space will look out of proportion and may lose their function. A too-large shrub might end up dark and uncomfortable to pass, while too-small shrubs purposely planted for screening will not work in that capacity.

Herbaceous perennials

Grand perennial expressions are best achieved when both depth and length of space are not an issue. In a successful perennial border, plants complement each other in the best way possible, both in terms of their appearance and how they change over the course of a season. Some perennials are sturdier than others, and some appear very heavy when holding their flowers – herbaceous peonies as a typical example. To plan a scheme where plants naturally support each other will help them look at their best; this is preferable to adding stakes and metal supports. By placing lower-growing species in the foreground, and gradually specifying taller plants towards the centre or back, a natural support will be given to the structure.

Conifers

Conifers were immensely popular in Scandinavia in the 1970s. Unfortunately, they were sometimes over-used and left to grow too large, which has led to an undeserved bad reputation. Used appropriately, they can be wonderful architectural plants – steadfast in form, gently scented, easy to maintain and evergreen. *Picea abies* 'Little Gem' is a versatile low, compact spruce, perfect for the small garden, while *Juniperus communis* 'Hibernica' works well as a tall, columnar specimen or mixed in a border. As much as bare deciduous trees give strength to a garden in winter, conifers add richness and balance, as well as reflecting the wider landscape.

Fleeting blooms
—
Opposite: The plants we prefer is subjective, and of the ones that affect us the most, we prefer them in their blooming state, even if this occurs only for a short time. Apple, cherry and pear all carry fragile and particular expressions when in bloom, as here in Ystad, Sweden. The vitality and beauty is like a silent strength when they stand before us, covered in blossom. They speak to us with hope, and are common in many gardens in Scandinavia.

Making variation work
—
This border by Zetterman Garden Design in Roslagen, Sweden features variation in shapes, heights and colour. Height is provided in the centre by the use of the oval-leaved *Cotinus coggygria* 'Royal Purple', which also provides a striking focal point through its maroon colour. The shrub is surrounded by lower perennials such as the funnel-shaped flower heads of *Hemerocallis* 'Pardon me' and bundles of buttons of *Astrantia major* 'Roma'. Lower perenials are used close to the stone, such as *Heuchera* 'Chocolate Ruffles', and the mass of heart-shaped green leaves of *Epimedium × perralchicum* 'Fröhnleiten' are distributed repeatedly and systematically. Scattered throughout the scheme the deepest and darkest foliage recurs: *Actaea ramosa* 'Brunette'.

Combining the subtle and the bold
—
Changes in a planting composition may be subtle or bold, yet all provide interest. In this border by Tidens Stauder Design in Sealand, Denmark, the strikingly dark and heavy *Sedum* 'Jose Aubergine' gives stature to the border, communicating with the dark stalks of *Salvia nemorosa* 'Caradonna'. *Eryngium planum*, on the other hand, provides a more subtle change of rhythm, through its slightly taller but small oval flower heads, contrasting in shape to the other slender plants.

Mixing soft and hard characters

—

Opposite, above Plants can have woody and hard stems, or weak and soft ones, which determines how straight and sturdy they are. This garden in Djursland, Denmark, by Kjeld Slot of Haver & Landskaber, is called 'The golden cut' and contains yellow plants, *Alchemilla mollis* included, running down a narrow axis. *Alchemilla* is soft in character and tends to fall gently when mature and in bloom, which can be useful when a comforting and tranquil effect is desired.

Coastal inspiration

—

Opposite, below: This planting by Tidens Stauder Design in Sealand, Denmark was inspired by sweeping coastal dunes, and incorporates blue grasses such as *Leymus arenarius* 'Blue Dune', *Festuca glauca* 'Intense Blue' and sea kale, *Crambe maritima*. Both *Leymus arenarius* and *Crambe maritima*, as well as varieties of *Festuca* grow in the wild in Scandinavia. By grouping plants in large clusters, shapes and colours become prominent, with the deep blue *Salvia × sylvestris* 'Viola Klose' used repeatedly, representing ocean waves and linking to the sky.

Traces of heritage

—

Plants come with their own history, and there are many treasures to be found in inherited gardens. Traces of the past can sometimes be found in the wider landscape, too, such as apple trees or daffodils. *Lilium martagon* is a heritage plant found in old and new gardens alike, as here in Stockholm, Sweden. The tall plant is majestic in a garden with its softly backward-curved petals and rich orange anthers.

Abstract shapes
—

Plants convey moods in a garden, but so do more abstract shapes. This scheme by Zetterman Garden Design in Saltsjö Duvnäs, Sweden is very organized, using precise gestures. Planting in squares and the use of several units creates an echo across the surface, with the last unit as a strict landing piece, enclosed by granite paving on all sides, while the first three are connected to the wooden walkway and the loose gravel.

*Viewing planting
from indoors*
—

In this house in Saltsjö Duvnäs, Sweden, generous windows frame the garden and with interesting planting, views can be fascinating at any time of year. The planting outside this window, by Zetterman Garden Design, contains a lot of fine foliage, using *Artemisia ludoviciana* 'Silver Queen', *Hemerocallis* 'Green Flutter' and *Trollius* 'Alabaster'. and appearing busy and lively compared with the more solid and sober effect indoors.

Geometric planting
—

Planting can be used as a geometric device, with groups planted in circles and squares, and with interesting angles. This can enhance the shapes of the hard landscaping or add new shapes to invigorate the design. The low shrubs planted in this garden in Oslo, Norway by Østengen & Bergo Landskapsarkitekter use an angle rather than a perpendicular line, breaking the regularity of the straight lines, and leading the eye in a new direction.

*Array of contrasting
shapes*
—
This combination of
plants in a garden in
Sealand, Denmark by
Tidens Stauder Design
shows strong variation
in terms of contrasting
shapes, through the
slender leaves of *Iris
sibirica* 'Perry's Blue'. This
is combined with the less
prominent button-shaped
flowerheads of *Achillea
millefolium* 'Terracotta'
and the prolific *Nepeta ×
faassenii* 'Walker's Low'
with its masses of flower
spikes.

*Considering height
and spread*
—
Height and spread
are important design
considerations. Each
plant should be planned
for and used to its
advantage. Working
with foliage in a cascade
is most successful when
lower plants are used
close to the edge of a
border, as here in a
garden in Roslagen,
Stockholm by Zetterman
Garden Design. By taking
this approach plants
will support each other
and each plant will be
clearly visible. Taller
plants may have a
rather uninteresting
base so lend themselves
to being covered by
lower-growing species.

*Common wild flowers
for effect*

—

The *Trollius* used in
this garden by Zetterman
Garden Design in
Svinninge, Sweden is
common in many parts
of Scandinavia, and
is closely related to
Ranunculus acris, found
in wild meadows. Here
Trollius chinensis 'Golden
Queen' provides welcome
colour and lightness in
the strict design, just as
Papaver and *Aquilegia*
would do in an early
summer garden scheme.

Meadow planting
—

A well-balanced meadow, as here in Saltsjö Duvnäs, Sweden, created by Zetterman Garden Design, contains both grasses and flowering plants, which together make a good wildlife habitat and are also aesthetically pleasing. A meadow can give a garden a very free-flowing expression, and can fit in small or large areas. To stand quietly in the middle of a meadow in summer and just listen and observe, gives access to a whole world of life bursting into the space. Every butterfly, ladybird, bee, grasshopper and beetle seems to be working as if there is no tomorrow.

A reminder of the country
—

There are many reasons to include a meadow in a garden: the soil might be difficult, or the elevation of the site awkward. In a city garden, such as this one in Saltsjö Duvnäs, Sweden by Zetterman Garden Design, it can provide a reminder of the wild and help preserve wild plants, which might otherwise be forgotten or even disappear from our landscapes.

New combinations
—
As much as garden design is about responsibility and the appreciation of nature, it also enables creativity. In this scheme at the Chelsea Flower Show, London, UK by Darren Saines Hagedesign AS, traditional species are used, but with a selection of varieties and in an arrangement not seen together in nature. This composition was created as a modern approach to using old plants, containing dark *Aquilegia vulgaris* var. *stellata* 'Black Barlow' and light blue *Meconopsis betonicifolia* softly embedded in *Stipa tenuissima*.

The position of strong shapes is an important consideration, as in this otherwise free-flowing scheme by Tidens Stauder Design in Sealand, Denmark. The two *Buxus* spheres, resting on a sturdy timber frame in the front of this border, provide stability, seemingly to anchor the border in place. Their size allows for the artistic flair of perennials and grasses to show off around them, yet they also seem to reach out to the back of the border with their warm green, connecting with the equally uplifting solid green conifers.

Symmetrical approach
—

Right: In this symmetrical approach by Tidens Stauder Design in Sealand, Denmark the same plants occur on both sides of the path. The *Hydrangea arborescens* 'Annabelle' provides strong visual impact, with its large, globe-shaped flower heads contrasting with the airy and light spires of *Persicaria amplexicaulis* 'Alba'. The shapes of the leaves are varied and repeated throughout the base and front of the border, providing interest for many months, with plants such as *Hosta fortunei* 'Patriot', *Sedum erythrostictum* 'Frosty Morn', *Brunnera macrophylla* 'Mr Morse' and *Alchemilla mollis*.

Hedging as a design element
—

Above: This garden in Saltsjöbaden, Stockholm by Zetterman Garden Design uses hedging as a backbone of the design, not only in the perimeter, but within the central space itself. Taller hedges frame the back of the space with a lower hedge running perpendicular, briefly seen in the rear, while the third, lowest hedge, frames the planting close to the house. Existing trees and taller shrubs were retained on both sides of the garden to provide intimacy to the space and frame the view beyond..

Incorporating trees
—
Trees should always be selected with care, considering shape and size, and should be appropriate to the situation, both for visual interest and in order for the tree to thrive. Given that many of us have limited garden space, small and cone-shaped trees can be considered and perhaps roof-pleached trees, as used in this garden by Have- og Landskabsarkitektfirmaet AT ApS and Arne Thomsen in Vejle, Denmark. The narrow and strict canopy of the *Platanus acerifolia* makes the trees stand as sculptures in the space, accompanied by a round *Buxus sempervirens* 'Rotundifolia'. The greenery is enhanced by bringing the planted sections into the patio.

Opposite: A granite stone path accentuates the planting and makes a steep slope look more natural.

Right: *Rosa* 'Ghislaine de Féligonde' with apricot-coloured buds opening to creamy white flowers is in flower for a long time, from July until October.

Planting to honour Swedish heritage and wildlife

—

Roslagen, Sweden
Design by: Zetterman Garden Design
4500m²

Scandinavia is spacious, with many farms and houses in the countryside enjoying large gardens. These gardens can often be very old, containing plants, fruit trees and berry bushes, which have been there for decades. This country garden was designed with an appreciation for the world of plants and our wildlife, with the aim of cultivating both the soil and our heritage. A priority in this garden was that it remained in keeping with the style of the house and its surroundings, only working with natural stone and with an array of mainly warm plant colours – yellows, oranges, reds, pinks and magentas – making the garden feel friendly and happy. Seasonal variations were important to this family, for the beds to provide habitat and food for bees and other insects all season as well as to satisfy a wish to pick flowers to use as interior decorations.

With a client interested in and knowledgeable about plants, discussions started over a cup of tea, looking through a set of images of favourite plants that had

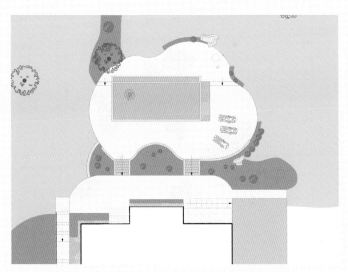

Plant list
—

Rudbeckia fulgida deamii
Physalis alkekengi franchetii
Paeonia lactiflora 'Buckeye Belle'
Artemisia stelleriana 'Morris Form'
Echinacea purpurea 'Tomato Soup'
Heuchera 'Beauty Color'
Helianthemum 'Orange Double'
Helianthemum 'Cerise Queen'
Echinacea 'Sunset' PBR
Echinacea 'Sunrise' PBR
Geum chiloense 'Mrs Bradshaw'
Helleborus orientalis 'Pink Lady'
Hemerocallis 'Pardon Me'
Hemerocallis 'Pink Damask'
Heuchera 'Marmalade' PBR
Heuchera micrantha 'Palace Purple'

Hosta 'Cherry Berry'
Iris germanica 'Apricot Silk'
Iris germanica 'Ola Kala'
Iris germanica 'Superstition'
Knautia macedonica 'Mars Midget'
Lilium 'Golden Splendour'
Miscanthus sinensis 'Dronning Ingrid'
Paeonia lactiflora 'Karl Rosenfield'
Paeonia lactiflora 'Pink Hawaiian Coral'
Persicaria affinis 'Superba' (Polygonum)
Sedum 'José Aubergine'
Sedum spurium 'Purpurteppich'
Deschampsia cespitosa 'Goldtau'
Achillea filipendulina 'Parker's Variety'
Anemone hupehensis 'Splendens'
Aquilegia 'Nora Barlow'
Astrantia major 'Claret'
Dicentra spectabilis 'Alba'

Hippophae rhamnoides 'Julia' E
Hippophae rhamnoides 'Romeo' E
Cotinus coggygria (Rub.) 'Royal Purple'
Fagus sylvatica 'Purpurea'
Rosa 'Ghislaine de Féligonde' (Moschata)
Rosa 'Louise Odier' (Bourbon)
Rosa 'Graham Thomas'

been collected in ring binders. With large areas and beds facing the sun in different directions, long lists of plants were created that could later be tweaked, once the layout plan was complete. When planning the layout of the garden, organic shapes were used in the scheme, to make the space feel more welcoming. Dimensions of the planting areas on the master plan were designed to be deep and wide, sometimes measuring as much as 5 × 10 metres, in order to obtain variation in the planting scheme.

Plants were planned to repeat throughout the scheme for a coherent look, yet not in an exact sequence in order to give the planting its natural and relaxed feel. Simple and ample expressions of flower heads were combined to provide differentiation and dynamics. Single examples of less pompous plants, for example *Aquilegia chrysantha* 'Yellow Queen' and *Geum chiloense* 'Mrs. Bradshaw', were selected, echoing the plants found in a wild meadow. These were mixed with flowers with an ample expression, such as *Rosa* 'Louise Odier'. Furthermore, foliage was carefully selected to have a lot of variation and colour, with numerous green tones as well as rich reds, purples and browns.

Plants that already existed such as peonies and day lilies were kept in the scheme, just like the fruit trees. The fruit garden has been extended with additional old varieties with proven qualities, such as *Malus domestica* 'Signe Tillisch' E and *Malus domestica* 'Gyllenkroks Astrakan' E. A plum tree was retained despite its poor condition, as it carried amazing fruit, and the seeds have now been recovered to give rise to new trees.

Opposite, above: Foliage covering the soil prevents weeds from taking root and supports neighbouring plants.

Opposite, below: A flower-shaped manhole cover made from limestone is a refreshing surprise among plants in this garden.

Right: A sturdy green foundation of ornamental grasses and *Hosta* are accompanied by the bright *Geum* 'Mrs J. Bradshaw' in summer, which loves full sun.

Below, left: *Rosa* 'The Pilgrim' is used as a climbing rose further south in Europe, but doesn't often grow that tall in Scandinavia, and is more usually used among perennials in this garden. It is in flower for most of the summer.

Below, right: A mixed border containing perennials, ornamental grasses, roses and shrubs provides interest all year round.

PALE

Using colour palettes for effect

A palette of pastels – dusty blue, soft yellow and powder pink, a dash of white and a hint of grey – this is the familiar perception of many when imagining typically Scandinavian colours. With the sunbeams at a very low angle, the colour spectrum occurring in the Scandinavian landscape often holds a range of what our eyes interpret as chalky pastels, and much less of the pure, intense and solid colours we might see further south. The soft light makes very fine detailing easy to see, such as surface textures, delicate flowers and the structure of grasses.

Colour is everywhere around us and has a great impact on our emotions; sometimes more than we might be aware of. For example, gardens that contain a lot of soft landscaping and green make us feel relaxed and comfortable. Colour is also part of our cultural heritage. In Scandinavia colour choices reflect our identity; values based around simple, sober expressions, relating to what we see in the landscape, our surrounding seas, and our mountains.

Colour characteristics

Simply stated, when light hits our eyes, our brain translates what we see, resulting in part in the perception of colour. Colour is complex, and affects us in ways we are not always aware of. We often put names to colour when trying to explain its endless variations, such as 'lemon yellow', 'olive green' or lavender blue'. There is a reason we feel free when looking at a blue sky, sending out its message of calmness and trust, or why we feel uplifted by the vivid red colours of autumn; red communicates energy. Colour have a profound impact on our mood, and perhaps the muted colours we see in Scandinavia make us somewhat less expressive … but also less temperamental.

Colour is everywhere in a garden – in hard landscaping such as paving, wood and gravel, and in soft landscaping such as foliage and bark. These colours should be carefully considered, given that they represent much of what we see throughout the seasons. Bear in mind that when talking about 'colour' in a garden we are often referring specifically to flowers in bloom; the flower heads rather than the foliage. There is a reason why foliage is green and why flower heads are not: the two components have completely different functions. While foliage contains green chlorophyll, absorbing energy from the sun to enable the plant to grow, flowers attract pollinators, and sometimes form camouflage to protect themselves.

The colours we find appealing and those we find repulsive come down to individual preference. Generally, red is seen as a dominant, energetic colour that stands out in a garden and comes forward, while orange is warm, and yellow can be intense, yet happy. By contrast blue opens up a space, connects with the sky and water and is much less commanding. Green makes us relax; gardens containing lots of green tend to appear comforting.

Emotive colour
—

Few things influence our emotions as strongly as colour in a design. Knautia are ideal to use when slender height is desired, as in this garden by Zetterman Garden Design in Roslagen, Sweden. With their small button heads and fine foliage they work as interlocking plants, with other sturdy plants at the base, providing soft movement through their long, bare stalks. This composition is made both dreamy and enticingly deep, through the maroon-red *Knautia macedonica* and the vulnerable pale-violet *Knautia arvensis*.

Fragile flowers
—
Blueberry flowers don't just appear fragile – they really are exceptionally delicate. The flowers of *Vaccinium myrtillus*, seen here in Uppsala, Sweden, appear in May and June – but one single night of frost is all that is needed for the harvest to be lost. The flowers are a harmonious blend of washed-out pink and turquoise, the embodiment of calm, sweet and refreshing in our landscapes, and perfect for incorporating into gardens with a naturalistic aesthetic.

Colour has many characteristics. First, a colour has a hue, defining the colour itself, such as yellow, blue or red. Second, a colour can be more or less intense, for which we use the word saturated. The colour of *Papaver orientale* 'Beauty of Livermere' is an example of a pure, highly saturated colour. Furthermore, value refers to the lightness or darkness of a colour. Combining colours with different values – different lightness and darkness – gives depth in a space. Pastels, commonly found in the Scandinavian landscapes, often contain white and sometimes a tone of both white and black, appearing less intense and softer than a pure colour such as that in *Campanulas*, *Trifolium pratense* and *Lonicera periclymenum*. Plants and flowers that are dark contain additional black, a so-called shade, appearing rich, mystical and powerful in gardens – such as *Lilium* 'Landini'.

Allowing for further categorization, a colour can be warm or cold. Warm colours make a planting appear to come close and seek attention, while cold colours tend to have a receding and calming effect. Colours with different temperatures may appear fascinating – or odd. Some feel that a pink colour containing yellow, perceived as warm, combined with a pink colour containing blue, perceived as cold, does not resonate well. For example, combining the warm *Paeonia lactiflora* 'Coral Charm' with the cold pink *Echinacea purpurea* may have this effect. Others might find the combination vivid and interesting. *Paeonia lactiflora* 'Coral Charm' combined with a peacefully united yellow plant such as *Hemerocallis lilioasphodelus* is a less controversial choice, as they have the same temperature and degree of warmth.

Depending on the message you want to communicate across a garden, colours can be combined with very little, or very strong contrast. For a considerable, sometimes dramatic, colour effect, combinations such as blue and orange or purple and yellow are worth trying. For a calm and mild effect you might want to consider combining colours that are similar, such as purple and blue, providing little in the way of divergence.

What colour goes where in the garden and to what extent a colour is used, should also be considered. Using dark colours in a shady spot or an enclosed area may result in them not being visible, making the space even darker, while a white monochrome planting and brighter materials, reflecting a lot of light, could be appropriate. On the other hand, a lot of white and solid bright colours in open spaces with direct sunshine might get lost, with too much light reflecting away.

Colour combinations

Scandinavians really appreciate the light, and perhaps that is why we tend to use a lot of pale colours in our designs. Generally speaking, gardens contain a colour palette for each season, with the most neutral palette in winter, of dead seed heads and brown bark. There are no rules, only guides, when it comes to using colour in a garden. You might find inspiration in the local surroundings, in the sea next to a coastal garden or in the wall next to a city garden. By studying and looking at plants you will gain an understanding of their properties and start to create your own artistic palettes. Be firm about what you want to communicate when selecting colours. A friendly cottage garden might contain a lot of variation, while a strict scheme will contain fewer colours. Also think about what emotions you want to bring out in the space: should it be warm and cheerful, containing a lot of yellow, or calm and cool, containing blues … or both?

Colour is a dynamic tool. Colours interact with each other in a garden and the balance this provides to the space helps to lead the eye and give the garden its character. Some gardens have a high degree of variation in colour, resulting in a rapid rhythm and a busy impression

The power of red
—
Red is an intense, passionate colour, the complementary of green which makes red flower heads so pronounced against their foliage. Red can evoke power and even aggression, but also lust, desire and heat. As summer fades into autumn the production of chlorophyll stops for deciduous plants, uncovering the red pigment. In this garden in Saltsjöbaden, Sweden by Zetterman Garden Design the saturated red palmate leafs of this *Acer palmatum* 'Osakazuki' look radiant and sensational in autumn.

in the space, while a low frequency makes the rhythm comparatively slow.

Depending on your colour combinations and the amount of particular colours used, a certain colour can make another seem intensified or toned down. For instance, when using purple and orange, larger amounts of purple than orange will tone down the orange, which otherwise tends to stand out and be more prominent than purple. Darker colours give depth and can be used as a backdrop to help another, lighter colour to stand out. It is not only the colour that determines the effect in a border, however, but the size of the area. If plants are modest and delicate, a large number over a wide area may be needed to provide a strong effect, such as masses of small flowers in a wild flower meadow.

Subtle verticals
—
Colours can change how we perceive shape, toning down a forceful expression where necessary. *Lupinus polyphyllus* is a plant commonly seen at the peak of summer in Scandinavia, in gardens and wild landscapes alike. It is perhaps one of the most resolute verticals that thrives in the far north. With their sculptural shapes and fine, clear colours, mainly purples, pinks and whites, they become gentle despite their vigour, as here in Dalarna, Sweden.

Opposite: When working with white plants in particular, an understanding of how light behaves is useful. Selecting white might seem simple, until you analyse the numerous undertones that white can show, depending on the light. A white can look dull ,with undertones of grey, or dusty, with undertones of yellow. These lily-shaped *Tulipa* 'White Triumphator' in full bloom appear very clean and light in this composition by Tidens Stauder Design in Sealand, Denmark. However, they are accompanied by *Brunnera macrophylla* 'Betty Bowring' with their warm green foliage.

Relaxed and dream-like
—
Playing with colour in garden design encourages creativity. Blues and purples were used in this informal garden by Zetterman Garden Design, close to the sea in Värmdö, Sweden, to make the garden seem relaxed and dream-like. *Nepeta racemosa* 'Superba' and *Salvia × sylvestris* 'Rose Queen', both containing white, provide little divergence in colour, and their similar slim and loose appearance gives a sense of informality to the space.

Achieving contrast is
a priority when creating
monochrome borders
to keep them from
appearing monotonous.
This border by Tidens
Stauder Design in
Sealand, Denmark
springs off from the idea
of mixing drought-
resistant perennials and
grasses in a monochrome
colour scheme of white.
It demonstrates the
importance of the shape
and stature of adjacent
plants, as colour can
provide little divergence.
The foliage is pale too,
containing tints of white,
harmonizing with the
white flower heads.
The greatest contrasts
can be found in the
shapes, in particular the
globe thistle *Echinops
sphaerocephalus* 'Arctic
Glow', which breaks up
the pattern with its bold,
spherical shape.

Bold orange
—
Orange plants in a garden in Svinninge, Sweden command attention, but in a gentler way than red flowers would. An orange plant containing white such as *Potentilla × tonguei* is calming and consoling, while a golden and pure orange such as this *Trollius chinensis* 'Golden Queen' seems to suggest wealth, happiness and wisdom through its clear, confident colour.

Working warm colours into a scheme
—

Warm colours in a garden tend to come forward, while cold colours recede. The warm pink of the schizocarps of *Acer tataricum ssp. ginnala*, seen here in Vallentuna, Sweden, is further accentuated by sunbeams hitting it, and reflecting light off the glossy surrounding foliage. The schizocarps connect to the warm green foliage to give a general welcoming appearance. Later in the season, *Acer tataricum ssp. ginnala* turns a deep and vibrant red, evoking a completely different set of emotions.

Variegated bark
—
Plant knowledge will free you up to experiment with planting, and exploiting the colour of foliage, bark, stems and flowers providing scope for even more artistic flair. Deciduous trees are ideal for smaller gardens and spaces, such as *Maackia amurensis* 'Summertime', covered in mottled olive green and golden bark, or *Acer pensylvanicum fk. Västeråker E*, dressed in white-striped bark, as seen here in Saltsjö Duvnäs, Sweden. Both have ornamental value in a garden all year around.

Bold combinations within a single plant
—

Left: Plants can marry several surprising colours, such as *Iris* 'Carnaby', *Primula vialii* and *Hemerocallis* 'Stafford', and this characteristic can be useful when matching them with other plants that contain similar colours. *Echinacea purpurea* 'Magnus' appears flamboyant by combining cold pink petals and a warm amber-coloured centre, giving it a fascinating dual personality, as seen here in Rönninge, Sweden.

Exploiting complementaries
—

Above: Saturated orange in the *Papaver pseudo-orientale* combined with equally saturated purples in the salvias and lupins in this scheme in Roslagen, Sweden by Zetterman Garden Design make a big impact, working as complementary colours. This apparent randomness and informal pattern in fact communicates with the surroundings and colours associated with the house, such as the orange roof tiles, as well as white and green in the detailing of the timber façade.

Changing colour intensity
—
Flower heads change in colour intensity from when they first bloom to when they are about to die back. This planting in Sealand, Denmark, by Tidens Stauder Design, is seen here peaking during early summer, when the self-seeded *Papaver somniferum* 'Claus Dalby' is accompanied by *Salvia nemorosa* 'Amethyst'. The two are closely related in colour, while they elegantly contrast in shape. The *Papaver* has a white tint in its foliage, making the flowers seem richer and accentuated, while the texture and colour of the white *Persicaria polymorpha* combine to provide a clean and refreshing backdrop.

Unusual combinations
—
Colour combinations that we don't see very often may appear surprising. In this summer display by Zetterman Garden Design in Roslagen, Sweden, colours are saturated and rich, with flowers creating strong contrasts. The larger flower heads of the red *Helenium* 'Rubinzwerg' provide strength, communicating with the maroon *Knautia macedonica* through its shape while they contrast in colour. The yellow *Achillea filipendulina* 'Parker's Variety' provides a cheerful splash of yellow. The brown centre part of the *Helenium* 'Rubinzwerg' provides depth and seems to ground the composition.

*Coherence in a
pale scheme*
—
In this planting in Jutland,
Denmark by Kjeld Slot
of Haver & Landskaber,
pale verticals provide
volume. The upright
yellow *Phlomis russeliana*
and the spikes of
Verbascum chaixii are
linked through their
light colour and upright
appearance. From a
distance, the foliage of
Deschampsia cespitosa
'Bronzeschleier' inclines
towards yellow, bringing
a sense of happiness to
the back of the border
and connecting with the
perennials through the
colour of its foliage.

Delicate pale purple
—
A pure hue of purple, using red and blue, is associated with nobility and ambition, with deeper shades often seen as magic or mysterious. Purples that contain white, however, signal a completely different message associated with delicacy and grace – think of *Lavandula* or *Syringa vulgaris*. The dark contrasting backdrop for this *Veronicastrum*, seen in Kalmar, Sweden, is a dark green solid wood panel, which makes the pale colour come forward in this planting.

*Assertive colours
and shapes*
—
Lively colour can send
an even stronger message
when paired with a
forceful shape. The joyful
Kniphofia 'Alcazar' does
justice to its common
name, 'torch lily'. With
robust upright stems and
vivid pointy flower heads
it embodies enthusiasm
in an autumnal border
in Roslagen, Sweden
by Zetterman Garden
Design. Other upright
plants similar to
Kniphofia in shape,
though less saturated
and containing tints of
white, are varieties of
lupins, delphiniums
and *Aconitum*.

121

Burst of bold colour

—

Colour bursting out quickly in a strong mass, destined to bloom and fade just as quickly can be refreshing and exciting. In this garden in Sealand, Denmark, by Tidens Stauder Design – normally referred to as 'The White Alley' – the *Laburnum × watereri* 'Vossii' completely dominates the garden when in bloom. The magnitude of colour and energy that fills the space is beyond words, and the otherwise obvious whites have to make way during this time. The mass planting of white *Anthriscus sylvestris* 'Ravenswing' seems not to compete with the overwhelming intensity, but instead accentuates the yellow.

123

Playing with colour relationships
—

For this seaside garden by Zetterman Garden Design in Värmdö, Sweden, colour was chosen to connect to the summer-blue skies and the water, and to look natural, yet also to provide divergence. *Perovskia* 'Blue Spire', containing both blue and purple and the same amount of white, relates to the very similar colour of *Geranium* 'Rozanne'. The ruby-red *Hemerocallis* 'Pardon Me' and the *Achillea millefolium* 'Red Velvet' work closely in the same way. The contrast is achieved by the blues being light and containing white, while the reds are darker, containing a shade of black.

Luminous, saturated yellow

—

Yellow is the most luminous of all colours when saturated, just like the sun itself. This late-blooming *Clematis tangutica* in a garden in Saltsjöbaden, Sweden by Zetterman Garden Design can be used as a refreshing addition both in late summer and early autumn. In this garden it has a black pergola as support, making a strong contrast with the flowers so they are easy to see. The yellow flowers are accompanied by spherical seed heads that appear as a cluster of silver feathers.

Tender pastels

—

Embracing the light, and aiming for bright and simple creations are attributes often connected with Scandinavian design and aesthetics. Pastels and washed-out, milky colours, sometimes with fine textures, become more apparent in the fragile light of the far north. This *Paeonia mascula*, seen in Stockholm, Sweden, evokes tenderness through its simple, delicate petals and pale colour.

Evolving colours
—
Flowers can show
different colours and
send different messages
depending on their stage
of development. The
flowerheads of *Echinops
ritro* 'Veitch's Blue', seen
here in Helsinki, Finland,
possess this particlar
depth just before they
bloom. Dark indigo blues,
very deep and rich, are
often perceived as
sophisticated and elegant.
Meanwhile a flowering
Echinops ritro 'Veitch's
Blue' is much paler,
filled with abundant
light steel-blue flowers
around its spherical body,
appearing much lighter
and gentler, and also
attracting butterflies.

An array of pinks
—
This planting in dry
and sandy soil in Sealand,
Denmark by Tidens
Stauder Design is a
veritable pink heaven.
In this scheme two
Echinacea varieties
work hand in hand, with
the lighter *Echinacea
purpurea* 'Magnus',
containing more white,
and the saturated
Echinacea purpurea
'Pica Bella'. The petals
of both varieties contain
blue; they have the same
colour temperature but
are not equally saturated.
The warmth from the
cone-shaped inner part
links to the foliage of
the cherry tree, *Prunus
cerasifera* 'Nigra'.

Plant list (selected)
—

Sesleria nitida

*Molinia caerulea
ssp. arundinacea*
'Transparent'

Salvia × sylvestris
'Rose Queen'

Echinacea 'Green Jewel'

Calamintha nepeta

Scabiosa 'Butterfly Blue'

Astrantia major

Geranium sanguineum
'Apfelblüte'

Hosta 'Frances Williams'

Allium Christophii

Hemerocallis
'Joan senior'

Nepeta superba

Spiraea japonica
'Little Princess' E

Kolkwitzia amabilis
'Kellokas'

Rosa rugosa
'Fru Dagmar Hastrup'

Rosa 'Rhapsody in
Blue Frantasia PBR'

Prunus pumila depressa

Hydrangea paniculata
'Limelight'

Clematis 'Nelly Moser'

Clematis
'Mrs T. Lundell' E

Lavandula augustifolia
'Hidcote'

A colour palette to express Swedish coastal living

—

Värmdö, Sweden
Design by: Zetterman Garden Design
1600m²

This seaside garden, looking on to the archipelago outside Stockholm which buffers the area from the open Baltic Sea, rests on an esker with sandy soil and tons of rather large cobblestones, which have been washed and polished by the ocean since the last Ice Age.

The space had to fulfil several purposes, including providing an easy and convenient parking space and entrances from an upper level and a lower level to the property, as well as a pleasant front garden. Furthermore, the intent was for the garden to express coastal living, with a chilled and friendly atmosphere of timeless appeal, including favourite colours of purple and pink.

Opposite: The purple semi-double flowers of *Rosa* 'Rhapsody in Blue' convey a sense of strength, yet also vulnerability.

Above: A simple frame with drapes of clematis will act as a decorative backdrop to a small seating area.

Right: Granite setts in a segmental arc pattern lend softness to the scheme, resonating with the natural granite wall.

This part of the garden is exposed; basking in the sun in summer and being highly light-reflective with the sea so near. Hence both hard and soft landscaping were designed in moderate colours – with neither the very dark shades which would get very hot, nor bright whites, which would reflect too much light. The approach was to use materials influenced by the coastline, and make the garden visually connect to the water. Large round and ellipse-shaped boulders were incorporated into the scheme. These were found on site, so they fitted in well. Placed among planting, they play an important role in providing support and changing the rhythm of the plants as well as being visually interesting in winter, when many of the perennials die back. These granite stones create a natural look in the terrain, both in their shape and in their sandy colour, just like the sand on a beach.

The colour palette of the planting uses pale cream, yellow, blue, purple, pink and variations in the foliage from fresh to sea-foam greens to evoke the water, the sky and the lush lawn, which are all viewed from this side of the garden. Solid borders of roses, *Rosa rugosa* 'Fru Dagmar Hastrup' and *Rosa* 'Rhapsody in Blue' and Frantasia (PBR), as well as *Lavandula angustifolia* 'Hidcote' provide soft and colourful harmonies with the natural stone walls and stairs. Perennial beds have been designed with organic outlines for a relaxed expression containing light and airy plants such as the purple *Salvia × sylvestris* 'Rose Queen' and blue *Scabiosa* 'Butterfly Blue' mixed with ornamental grasses in beds surrounded by sea shingle. *Hydrangea paniculata* 'Limelight' are planted in a shadier part of the space, shifting endlessly in a pale colour spectrum until winter hits and its bold flower head has transitioned into a sandy tone, contrasting with the snowy landscape.

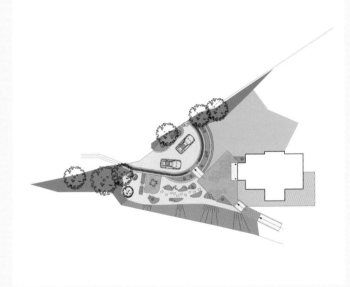

Opposite: A curved, irregular path slows down the pace of moving through the garden.

Right: Curved retaining walls filled with mass planting of roses and *Lavandula* form a gentle treatment for this slope, connecting visually with the granite rock in the background.

NAKED

Durability meets elegance in hard landscaping

Rumour has it that Scandinavians have a liberated frame of mind. We see no drama in the naturalistic – in fact, we adore all things natural and make them part of our everyday life. We like walking around barefoot in summer and will go for a swim in a nearby lake at the drop of a hat. We have an affection for stripping things back to the bare essentials. We often dress in clothes with clean lines (as long as they keep us warm in winter). We prefer to use plain language. Relatively speaking, we tend to be direct and open in conversation and the other ways in which we express ourselves.

We have a relaxed and close relationship with nature and natural materials, appreciating, for example, the honesty of bare wood where the grain is exposed. We embrace the character of rock formations where they emerge from the landscape. We work with materials to accentuate their positive characteristics, letting them speak for themselves in products and interiors, as well as in our gardens.

A natural landscape of bedrock and timber

Scandinavia is a region rich in resources, with stone and timber found everywhere apart from the very south, where the landscape is open and flat. Making use of natural materials has therefore been an important part of everyday life for centuries. We had to work hard to survive, and respect for natural materials and taking pride in our creations has always been a profound philosophy, which still holds true today. Innovation, and creating long-lasting products efficiently, were just as important in the old days: using stone for stable constructions, building houses of timber and carving cutlery from wood. A range of products and design classics such as chairs and tables created in the 1950s, when the design era was at its height, were also made from wood and steel, suitable for mass production. The same philosophy is applied to successful gardens and outdoor spaces in Scandinavia today, which are constructed with care in order to last, and make use of durable hard landscaping and dense stone and timber, to withstand the climate.

Gardens in the northern and central parts of Scandinavia often sit on bedrock on a hillside or include complicated rock structures in parts of the ground. Making use of steep elevations or bare rock and incorporating them into the design scheme can create a lot of character in the garden, with interesting divisions and unique sculptural features. By creating a relationship between already existing rocks and designed hard landscaping surfaces, a connection is created between the house and the garden, as well as with nature. The space is filled with contrasts between old and new, balancing the raw with more orderly and worked materials.

With dense forests in both Finland and Sweden and parts of Norway, wood in great quantities has been a common natural material to use for much of what we need; houses, domestic items and

parts of the garden, with timber panel fencing and screening, outdoor furniture and terraces being common. Wood, when compared to stone, is relatively soft and easy to work with, and consequently many bespoke structures and personal imprints can be readily created in a garden. Each piece has its own characteristics and detailing, bringing life and soul to the garden.

Designing using hard landscaping

Gardens that we create are here to stay for decades to come. How we use materials and change levels has a big impact on the mood of a garden, and it is wise to make a master plan showing the layout of the garden and the hard landscaping separately, before going into detail with the soft landscaping. The properties of a hard landscaping material are associated with many design considerations, taking into account its size, colour, patterning and surface texture. The palette of all hard landscaping materials should be carefully selected, from both a practical and an aesthetic perspective.

Function of hard landscaping

The mildest regions of Scandinavia are Denmark, southern Sweden and some coastal areas around Norway. Across the rest, toughness and endurance are key criteria for hard landscaping that can withstand the harsh climate of the north. Great variations in seasonal temperature mean that a dense stone is often needed to cope with our climate, while a porous stone might be too sensitive, and will break. When designing a composition it is helpful to look at the bare essentials – the needs, functions and logistics in the space – rather than making the garden design over-complicated or excessive in its use of hard landscaping materials. Surface textures with a good grip are essential for frequently used areas, on hills, slopes and flat surfaces alike. Hard landscaping for parking requires thought, as cars and heavy vehicles require material that can cope with heavy weights. Ensure that each hard landscaping surface fulfils its purpose and is used in proportion to soft landscaping. The size of seating areas and paths matter too: if they are too small, they lose both function and pleasure, and will feel cramped. A garden with too much hard landscaping may lead to a lack of balance with the soft landscaping, making it feel hard and sterile, and it may also result in a space with drainage problems.

Aesthetics of hard landscaping

In Scandinavia we often see beauty and decoration inherent to the material itself, which makes us very selective when choosing materials. This means we may find enough interest and variation even when using two different types of slate, for example. We favour function, and seldom dress or frame a material for decorative effect. Using an excessive range of different materials just because they are available does not necessarily lead to a better end result. To unify the space you might instead want to consider using fewer, carefully selected materials for the majority of surfaces. To work with these consistently through the space, with variation in size and surface texture, often gives enough variation to be aesthetically pleasing. This simple, honest approach we find encourages creativity in using materials in a garden.

How much variation you decide is appropriate in a garden design will depend on the effect you are aiming for. Sometimes a mixture of wood, stone and steel may suit, while other times timber or stone alone is the optimal option. The choice of materials should be based on what you want to communicate.

Large paving units make the surface seem calm, while smaller pavers provide patterns that are more pronounced and busy. It is wise to have a clear intention

Fitting in and making contrasts
—
Contrasting shapes and creative use of local materials can provide a garden with artistic flair that is still in keeping with its surroundings. This terrace by ARKÍS arkitektar, close to the Laki volcano in a moss-covered, lava-strewn landscape in Vatnajokulsthjodgardur, Iceland, uses gabions filled with local volcanic rock, creating a stunning contrast with the organic shapes of the natural surroundings. The gabions are visually powerful, and are also able to withstand the harsh and ever-changing weather conditions.

when working with hard landscaping, or
when changing level, material or direction,
to help the eye read the surface easily.
Remember too that the format of paving
slabs and the outline shape of a hard
landscaping area can either be organic
or geometric, giving yet more scope for
creativity. Organic shapes are perceived
as soft and gentle, while geometric shapes
and sawn faces reflect a garden that is
more strict and direct. Dynamics can be
achieved in either case.

The Scandinavian landscape contains
stone that is neither pure white nor pitch
black, but contains an array of more
neutral colours, including many greys
and browns. Think about texture, too:
textures with great variation may appear
too busy, while too little variation can be
tame and boring. The finish of the stone is
yet another aspect of what you choose to
communicate. Polished and highly glossy
stone is not found in nature, and may give
a garden a purposely manmade effect, but

equally it can look unnatural – a flamed
surface might be more appropriate. By
using a similar palette to what is found
in the surroundings, gardens that look
natural are also likely to communicate well
with other components such as the local
natural light quality, and plants indigenous
to the region. Temperature and light are
factors, too: dark horizontal surfaces can
be very hot to walk across, while over-
bright surfaces reflect too much light and
may be blinding.

Natural stone

Outdoor spaces created to harness the
qualities of natural stone are a beauty to
behold in a garden. There is such intricate
detailing and beauty in a natural stone,
each with its unique expression, and the
durability of natural stone cannot be
compared to any other hard landscaping
material. A long time ago, stone as a ground
covering was mainly reserved for towns,

Practical steps
—

Practical steps
—
Gardens in Scandinavia can be hilly, with steep slopes and paths, and access steps must be practical and sturdy. Using solid granite block steps may be worth considering, as they are highly durable and easy to maintain. With a flamed or bush-hammered surface they offer a good grip, and are suitable for use in steep stairs, in curved or straight lines, as well as by a front entrance, such as here in Värmdö, Sweden.

while gravel, as a less expensive option, was more often used in the country. Old dry stone walls can often be seen in the landscape, but now surround new gardens too. They were originally built where stones were naturally found in the ground to keep livestock enclosed and to protect them – as well as to mark out a plot of land. A dry stone wall seems to bring us closer to nature as well carrying on our traditions. By making elegant landscapes and gardens using natural stone we are reminding ourselves of our past, celebrating how our skilled craftsmen worked, and creating proud monuments to our future.

Granite

Granite is one of the most common rocks on Earth and can be found in almost all parts of Scandinavia, with most quarries situated in Finland and Sweden. Cobbled roads and granite setts can be found in most old towns, and are still widely used in new gardens and landscapes. Granite

has excellent qualities for use outdoors in Scandinavia, being very dense and therefore able to cope with severe weather conditions. The colour is determined by the combination of minerals, with the most seductive dark grey making gardens look exclusive, while mid-grey and red granites are more commonly used. Granite can be fairly small-grained, or may have larger and more varied textures, and can also be found in a range of surface finishes such as flamed, chiselled, bush-hammered and tumbled. It is versatile, comes in a range of sizes – from large blocks, used for steps and slabs, to smaller ones, used for stepping stones, setts and mosaics – and can be used for most purposes throughout a garden.

Slate

Just like granite, slate is an authentic material widely used in gardens in Scandinavia, with the majority of quarries found in Norway. Slate is ideal for many hard landscaping purposes in a garden, such as paving, steps and walls, and is often found as roof tiles in certain regions. Slate is composed of thin, but very strong, horizontal layers, densely compressed together, which gives it a unique aesthetic appeal when used in dry stone walling, with the thin layers and colour variations clearly visible. Slate can be applied with sawn edging for formality, or randomly laid with pavers in various sizes for a more spontaneous and informal look. Slate comes in a spectrum of colours, from the classic grey, to blue, green and red.

Limestone

There is a place in southeastern Sweden, on the island of Öland, called 'the Alvar'. An alvar is a limestone plain with often sparse vegetation, similar to a prairie. Next to Öland sits another island, Gotland, and the two islands are where most of the limestone in Scandinavia can be found. Limestone has been used for hundreds of years in the region, mainly in southern parts of Scandinavia, where the climate

*Making the most of
stone varieties*
—
The development of
quarrying techniques
has resulted in stone
becoming widely
available in a range of
types and dimensions.
This garden by Zetterman
Garden Design in Saltsjö
Duvnäs, Sweden uses
basalt for the sets while
the larger paving stones
are granite. These stones
have different mineral
compositions, resulting in
the granite displaying a
light grey colour, while
the basalt is much darker.
Basalt is very fine grained,
making the surface look
smooth and even.

is more temperate. Limestone, being a soft stone, is appropriate for the conditions. Similar to granite and slate, limestone is used for multiple garden structures, walls and paving, in both formal and informal patterns. Limestone is matt and light in colour, so it appears very soft and smooth in a garden, with colours including grey, bone white, beige, red and brown.

Wood

Light, strong and naturally beautiful, timber is an old favourite that we still hold dear in the north. Timber is one of our greatest resources and has been an essential material in our culture and daily life for as long as anyone can remember, with furniture, everyday products and houses being made out of wood. Timber is both load-bearing and able to cope with the climate extremes, making it a very versatile, natural and popular material in Scandinavian gardens.

Timber is strongly directional, and often appears contemporary in gardens. A house made of timber can interact gracefully with structures made out of timber in the garden, sometimes seamlessly if they are in direct contact with the property. One of timber's many great qualities is that it allows for great creativity – it can be used for vertical, horizontal and oblique elements. Screening can be both functional and decorative, with a balance between mass and void in elegant semi-solid structures. Timber decking is comfortable to walk across and doesn't absorb heat in the same way as stone; it also provides great contrast with stone.

Steel

Materials that are not natural, such as concrete and steel, appear solid, flat and static by comparison. This can be an advantage with solid structures in a garden, which you also want to appear light, such as a bespoke trellis or a focal point to a wall. Corten steel has also become more popular in contemporary gardens, expressing a rustic, yet urban, look. Like stone and timber, steel is a material that can cope with the weather in the Nordic outback. Steel sheets cut thin can be used for formal or informal outlines, emphasizing shapes without dominating the space. While hard landscaping with sometimes dusky colours of stone and weathered timber may appear grey, corten steel provides welcome warm, brown shades.

Concrete

Concrete is composed of cement, sand and gravel aggregate. The possibilities to be creative with cast in-situ concrete are many, as more or less any shapes and structures can be made. Cast in-situ concrete structures do however require high standards of execution and a high-quality finish in order to look sleek and dignified in a modern garden, without any grouts or separate sections. Scale and proportion are crucial when working with cast in-situ concrete, as the surfaces – similar to steel – stand out as solid units. They clearly define space but don't blend into the landscape. Pre-cast concrete systems using voids that incorporate grass reinforcements are useful for parking spaces, helping water to drain and look gentler than large surfaces covered in paving only.

Gravel

Gravel can be sharp, crushed rock fragments, or soft shingle that has been smoothed by the waves for centuries. Gravel paths can be found in many old gardens in Scandinavia, as the material was affordable and accessible for agrarian farms and gardens. It was mainly used where functionality was important, such as for paths leading up to a house and other utility areas.

Gravel is well suited to many areas in a garden, and is often specified in informal schemes, providing a different look from solid hard landscaping surfaces. Gravel changes the mood and tempo in the space, relaxing it with its inherent looseness. Pockets of planting can be integrated to break up or soften the space further, with wiggly paths running in between. Just as with stone, gravel comes in different sizes with varying properties. Walking barefoot across gravel gives a different sensation from walking across solid paving – a more intense feeling, sometimes tingling, sometimes tickling, as well making a quiet crunching sound. Crushed gravel should be used when a good grip is required, as this doesn't move like a round stone, provided it is compacted and not too deep, in which case this function gets lost. Moreover, gravel helps drainage and can therefore be an excellent option for solid hard landscaping.

Naturalistic gravel
—
Decorative loose materials such as gravel and bark chippings work well in naturalistic gardens. Gravel gives a sense of softness, while bark chippings evoke woodland. Gravel can be used across large or small areas, and for paths or more ornamental parts of a scheme. The very fine gravel used in this garden in Sealand, Denmark by Tidens Stauder Design makes the space calm and quiet, blending with the soft landscaping for a remarkably tranquil overall effect.

Bold enclosing fence
—

People have marked out their plot of land since the earliest times, and you will find as many different enclosing structures as there are gardens. Sometimes wood fences reflect the character of the house, picking up on detailing from ornaments on the façade, and other times they are freestanding. This garden by Johan Sundberg Arkitektur in Kämpinge, Sweden is framed by horizontally arranged young spruce, stacked in its natural state with the bark left intact. The orderly and strict arrangement contrasts with the rustic, unfinished look to imbue the garden with real character.

Subtle and sparse detailing
—

Scandinavian design is characterized by sparse detailing. This is demonstrated in the delicate handling of the wood in this project by Gullik Gulliksen Landscape Architects in Sandefjord, Norway, with circular pieces of wood to cover the recessed screw holes in each board. The larger plank of wood placed between the pavers has been carefully crafted with angular edges. Detailing is subtle and shows appreciation for materials in their own right. Durable materials have been used for this garden, such as oak wood and Norwegian Alta slate.

*Expressing material
qualities*
—
Changing materials
without changing levels
seems to express the
material qualities more
clearly. In this garden
by Nygaard AS in
Stavanger, Norway,
the properties of each
material – textures,
colours and effect –
become evident. The
kebony wood offers a
lively and ornate look,
while the grainy surface
texture of the granite
pavers gives a cool
appearance that balances
well with its solid pattern
and square shapes.

Furnishing a landscape
—
Respecting not only the materials, but how they communicate with nature is important when designing a garden. With skilled craftsmanship, these stairs by John Robert Nilsson Arkitektkontor in Värmdö, Sweden, connect a series of footbridges and the landing stage at the front, with the effect of refined furniture in the landscape. The dignity of the ipe hardwood contrasts, and yet works in harmony, with the surroundings, by following a route that allows the stairs to hug the contours of the ground. By using a darker colour for the foundations of the stairs, the connection aspect becomes more pronounced, with the structural parts being less prominent.

Opposite: Scandinavians
have a profound liking
for outdoor showers, and
they are often seen in
gardens close to water.
It is also very convenient
when spending most of
the time outside in the
summer. An outdoor
shower doesn't have to
be hidden away in a
corner, but might be
placed more centrally
in a garden, where it is
convenient and could
act as a focal point.
In this fun design by
DesignHaver in Funen,
Denmark, a shower with
a slender pipe sharply
divides the heavy walls
of corten steel behind.

Unique stone patterning
—
Limestone is a
sedimentary stone
composed of remains
of marine life that shows
dramatic colour variations
and patterns. This
particular stone comes
from Gotland, an island
situated in the Baltic Sea,
where the bedrock is
connected to the sea
rather than the Swedish
mainland. Characterized
by endless variations
in texture and colour,
unique patterning in
each stone decorates this
garden in Saltsjöbaden,
Sweden by Zetterman
Garden Design.

Hard yet gentle
—
The power and solidity of hard landscaping contribute greatly to the emotions you choose to communicate in a space. Hard landscaping can be very gentle and yet still fulfil its purpose, such as this centrally placed fine structure. This gazebo by Tidens Stauder Design in Sealand, Denmark, made from rebars, stands majestically in the garden yet speaks quietly, balancing the sturdy green foliage of the *Fagus sylvatica* hedge, letting it dominate. Its circular movement and curves give it a soft and friendly appearance, in keeping with the shingle on the ground.

Informal expression
—
Informality in a garden
is often achieved through
the use of organic shapes
and irregular stones.
Here gravel is used, which
is naturally rather loose
and free, heightening
the informality and the
relaxed mood. In this
garden by Zetterman
Garden Design in Värmdö,
Sweden, informal curved
dry stone walls are used
as the backbone, with
the much smaller, round
sea gravel balancing and
softening the terraces,
as well as connecting to
the water close by.

Coherent concrete
—
This garden by Green Idea
in Ostrobothnia, Finland,
with its energetic and
joyful walls, is cooled
down by the light-grey
colour of the hard
landscaping. The
semi-open courtyard
retains its youthful
and eager expression
through a mix of wood
and concrete, with the
cast in-situ concrete
planter looking industrial
and sleek. The planter
frames the space as well
as performing a function
by marking the step, and
connects visually to the
cast concrete threshold
of the terrace.

Expressing materials and thickness
—

Using less of a material than is usual can create a striking effect. A clad wall can be created in which one side is faced, but the sides of the structure are left bare. By using this idea in this space in Aarhus, Denmark, DesignHaver used the slate cladding to give depth to the space while allowing materials and shapes to remain distinct, showing contrasting textures and thickness.

Guiding the eye
—

Breaking up a large space through the use of another material can help lead the eye towards a main entrance, such as in this garden in Stavanger, Norway by Nygaard. Kebony wood is used for the pathway, providing a functional walkway as much as it becomes a visual expression within the space. A sculptural element is created in the form of a concrete wall with voids, which catches the eye from an artistic perspective, but also functions as a screen to conceal what is inside.

Practical sculptural elements

—

Left: Sculptures in a garden add personality to the space. They often highlight areas from an artistic point of view, but they can also break up open spaces or signal awkward areas. At other times they might be multifunctional, such as the cast in-situ concrete benches used in this front garden by Gullik Gulliksen Landscape Architects, in Lysaker, Norway, which have a decorative quality underlined by the spherical sculpture at the end of one of the benches.

Terrace with a view

—

Below: Superbly located on a ridge with a magnificent panoramic view across a fjord in Asker, Norway, this scheme by Gullik Gulliksen Landscape Architects balances a classic and contemporary look. The dry stone wall, made from Oppdal slate, contains an array of colours, surface textures and patterns, balanced out by the more formal and calm surface of the terrace. The seamless glass screening provides sufficient shelter from winds and is also a safeguard, while still allowing maximum views.

Horizontal planes
—
This garden by
Zetterman Garden
Design in Ljunghusen,
Sweden makes use of
several horizontal planes.
By stretching them and
leaving them open they
function as steps, and yet
also work as a piece of art
in the space, rather than
mere stairs. The narrow
void under each plane
gives the appearance of
floating for a feeling of
lightness, which becomes
more pronounced when
they are illuminated
from underneath in the
evenings. The slightly
dark, diamond-polished
concrete surface gives the
garden a sense of dignity,
and also requires very
little maintenance.

Relaxed elegance
—
Combining clean, direct
lines with circular shapes
makes a space seem
orderly and soft at the
same time. In this garden
in Värmdö, Sweden
by Zetterman Garden
Design sawn faces make
this slate surface seem
controlled, but the circular
shape of the paving
gives a rather benevolent
and positive effect.
Low-growing perennials
and ornamental grasses
frame and soften the
circular shape but do not
suppress its elegance.

Calm simplicity
—
Opposite: This outdoor
spa area in a garden
in Sandefjord, Norway
by Gullik Gulliksen
Landscape Architects
is a place to unwind
and laze on a sunny
day, created with durable
materials including teak,
oak, slate and gravel.
Simplicity is inherent to
the long single lines of
oak wood running next
to the slate pavers, which
connect with the wooden
screen at the rear. The
generous size of the slate
pavers gives a sense of
calm, while the pergola
and wall structures use a
more energetic language
with their many narrow
boards. This simple
expression continues
in the planting, with
*Calamagrostis ×
acutiflora* 'Karl Foerster',
delicately screening off
the outdoor shower.

Common language
—
Gardens can incorporate
areas of distinctly
different expressions,
and yet remain coherent.
In this informal approach
by Zetterman Garden
Design in Värmdö,
Sweden, slate has been
used for the entrance,
in a random pattern,
to resonate with the
darker detailing of the
house and function well
in all seasons. The front
garden, situated next to
the entrance, is marked
by a granite stepping
stone path in a curving
line surrounded by sea
gravel, speaking the
same caring and
peaceful language as
the entrance, but using
different materials
and components.

Practical parking spaces
—
Parking spaces in gardens require special planning as they must withstand heavy loading. Large, solid areas may result in drainage problems and can also be out of proportion with the soft landscaping. This garden by Green Idea in Oulu, Finland makes use of a concrete paving grid system for grass reinforcement, allowing water to drain, and also forming a visually interesting, yet practical, space.

Directional wood
—

Opposite: Of all materials, wood is perhaps what most people think of when they think of Scandinavia. Wood is used in gardens across the entire region. It is a material that best suits our climate. Coming in long and narrow units, wood creates strong lines by its very nature, which should be exploited. A change of direction has a strong visual impact, leading the eye. In this garden in Kiðjaberg, Iceland by Minarc, vertical and horizontal planes create a continuous movement, clearly leading the eye in one direction.

Visual links on a grid
—

Playing with the scale and proportion of a grid using cast concrete elements can create great artistic effects. This front garden by Green Idea in Oulu, Finland uses a concrete paving grid system for grass reinforcement over a small seating area. This pattern is replicated across the lawn, which incorporates concrete slabs on the same grid, but on a much larger scale, linking the two areas visually.

Invitation to engage
—

Above: Scale and proportion not only provide balance and hierarchy, but can also make spaces seem more or less inviting. By stretching a platform across a silent water feature in this design by Piha- ja vihersuunnittelu Villa Garden in Li, Finland, a welcoming gesture to enter the space is extended, enhanced by the gentle shadows. The large square pavers signal trust by providing stillness in the pattern.

Linear expressions
—

Right: Subtle changes in hard landscaping provide variation while retaining a calm and sophisticated expression in this courtyard in Stockholm, Sweden by Zetterman Garden Design. This garden uses granite and diabase, both natural stones characterized by similar properties, being very dense and durable, but different in colour. Diabase is used as detailing, in a strict long strip across the garden floor in this scheme.

Scale and proportion
—

When working with hard landscaping in a garden, scale and proportion are important for function and aesthetics, and you might decide to change the rhythm within a space to add interest. This garden by DesignHaver in Aalborg, Denmark, uses a grid of soft lawn, oil-treated wood and granite. Strong contrasts are achieved by using black in the wood, which links to the still, dark water and the dark façade of the house. The use of equal widths and the direction of the wood and stone creates harmony in the horizontal flooring, with the gentle detail of the last row of paving interlocking and communicating with the raised surface.

Far left: Large polished gabbro pavers act as detailing and also suggest the direction of movement within the garden.

Left: In this garden soft landscaping is preserved and cared for as much as hard landscaping, with existing plants such as *Iris sibirica* standing tall, looking out over the fjord.

Below: Massive blocks of stone mark the entrance, enhanced by the light gravel that appears in the spaces inbetween.

Opposite: A dining and lounge area framed by seamless glass is protected from strong winds, but the barrier does not interfere with the mesmerizing views.

Plant list (selected)

—

Lilium martagon
var. *album*

Taxus × media
'Hillii'

Betula pendula
'Dalecarlica' E

Acer japonicum
'Aconitifolium'

Syringa vulgaris
'Mme Lemoine'

Prunus triloba

Rosa 'Lykkefund'

Rosa 'Rose de Rescht'

Hosta sieboldiana
'Elegans'

Tiarella cordifolia

Iris sibirica

Geranium renardii

Classic and contemporary Norwegian hard landscaping

—

Asker, Norway
Design by: Gullik Gulliksen
Landscape Architects
50,000m²

This residential garden is superbly located on a ridge with a magnificent panoramic view across the fjord towards the city of Oslo. It is a steep garden, with orchards and fields of perennials dropping down towards the fjord. The brief was to create a garden where classic meets contemporary with a strong aesthetic within the space, yet maintaining a natural look, in keeping with the surroundings. Generous spaces for multifunctional use were a priority, in which to socialize, relax and entertain.

The garden had tremendous landscape qualities from the very start, and it was key to maintain an exceptionally high standard of work at all times, in terms of materials and execution, as both the villa and parts of the garden are listed.

In such a large garden it was vital to create outdoor spaces with diverse qualities and with sufficient shelter from wind and weather, while also safeguarding

the view. Choices of stone and how they would be used were discussed early in the project. Genuine Norwegian Oppdal slate and river shingle were natural choices, resonating with the area. Detailing was proposed in basalt or gabbro, and the latter was decided on. The dimensions and positioning of this dark detailing were carefully planned. By using a polished finish in places, the stone is not only given a striking appearance, but also functions as a call for attention, enhancing elements such as benches and long lines leading in particular directions through the garden.

A large terrace was created for the main social area, facing east, overlooking the fjord. Dry stone walls and the floors on the terrace were meticulously implemented using both reclaimed and new slate, with the resulting colours naturally blending with the water and the sky. The terrace is divided into several zones, with a barbecue area, various residents' amenities, and a lounge area as well as smaller benches, from which to enjoy the view from every angle.

Parts of the planting in this heritage garden have been restored and replanted, with a huge, charming, old birch tree and sky-blue irises retained among other vegetation which was kept.

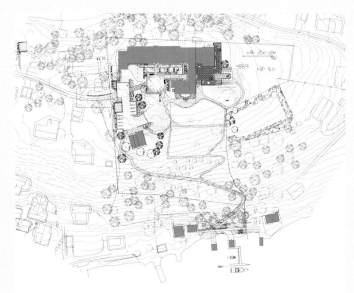

ATTUNED

Creative opportunities through the seasons

At first, Scandinavians might appear somewhat restrained; perhaps difficult to get to know. But put in some time and effort, and you might come to find us refreshing, stimulating and rather easy to be around. People's attitudes are often a reflection of their environment. The weather and temperature change almost daily, such shifts are reflected dramatically in the wide-open landscapes, and this in turn affects the people.

We live in a place where the full circle of life is exposed, feeling the fragile beginnings of spring, experiencing the vivid height of summer, fighting melancholy in autumn and witnessing mortality in winter … and then, after a long wait, we wake up once again to the first signs of spring.

Celebrating the seasons

The seasons are caused by the angle of the Earth's axis as it moves around the Sun. This affects how high the Sun rises above the horizon at different times of year, resulting in four distinct seasons in Scandinavia. The powerful seasonal variations strongly affect Scandinavians, evoking different emotions and forming a vital part of our culture in the Nordic outback. We celebrate the seasonal changes in our creative work and, put simply, they are the reason why we think, work and live the way we do.

Design in nature

Nature provides us with impeccably designed landscapes, from the finest detail of a leaf to the bigger picture of a sweeping vista. In some regions in Scandinavia pine trees tower majestically atop barren hills, while soft meadows lie innocently in valleys beneath. In other parts clusters of bell-shaped dancing spruces give rhythm to the forests between the watering holes of thousands of lakes, making up another distinctive and rich landscape. Here the visual density deadens every sound, and it is hard to break the silence.

Other regions are open and exposed, with carpets of sparse and low vegetation clinging on to the flatlands against the strong winds. Scandinavian nature amazes us all year round, constantly changing its character. Let's make gardens do the same!

There is much that we can learn from nature in terms of design detailing. If you are searching for ideas for structures and patterns, a walk in the outdoors may bring ideas uppermost in your mind: try observing and being open to the patterns of a pine cone, the sound of *Populus* swaying in the wind or the shape of a mountain … and see where it takes you.

Sumac in winter
—
Rhus typhina, or sumac trees, are either male or female, with fresh green foliage in summer turning into attractive shades of red, orange and yellow in autumn. The fruit forms dense clusters of large torch-like shapes lasting through winter and into spring in Scandinavia. Its architectural appearance with multiple stems makes it a prominent tree in a winter garden, as here in Oslo, Norway.

Sandy beaches, deep forests and bare tundra

If you don't know much about Scandinavia or plants, you might guess that it is a region with such a tough climate and relatively short summers that there is no point in caring about gardens. Hopefully this book provides evidence to the contrary! Climate determines what grows and how, and in all parts of Scandinavia, in every garden, despite the climate, there are many opportunities to make the space useful and inviting. And besides, the prevailing conditions in Scandinavia are distinctly different depending on the precise location.

The southern region, Denmark and southern Sweden, have a temperate climate, with temperatures that are relatively modest. They rarely experience extreme hot or cold, and there are often winters without snow, or with very little snow. The region is flat, with soils rich in humus, or sandy soils closer to the beach. Trees are mainly deciduous, such as beech, *Corylus* and *Quercus*. Plant choices are plentiful, and some plants grow enormous over time, such as varieties of magnolia, of which only a few thrive further north, and they don't reach nearly the same eventual height and spread.

Further north in Scandinavia the landscape contains many more dense and mixed forests, mainly dominated by *Picea*, *Pinus* and *Betula*. Soils are varied, with some containing more clay, and beaches have been replaced by cliffs along the shoreline. Thousands of lakes spread across vast areas in a rather dense landscape in Finland and Sweden, while the seas of the west coast of Norway have extended into deep fjords, elongated and narrow between towering mountain walls. Gardens show distinct seasonal changes, with constant snow cover in winter.

In the far north, in Lapland, spaces are barren and open. These regions can suffer extreme winds and unpredictable, drastic weather changes. The inland climate in Sweden and Finland can reach severe lows in winter, with records of -50°C, and it is very tough for any plant to survive, with the richer flora in lower valleys. Alpine plants and moss are suited to these regions, as plants which don't have root systems that reach deep down, as the ground can be cold even in summer. Examples of such plants are *Dryas octopetala*, *Gentiana nivalis*, *Saxifraga oppositifolia* and *Silene acaulis*.

Along the coast of Norway, as well as in many parts of Iceland, winds affect the landscape too, but fortunately these regions of Scandinavia in particular benefit from the Gulf Stream, which tempers the climate. In this maritime climate temperatures are never extremely cold in winter, and summers are cool rather than hot. These conditions, coupled with open landscapes with strong winds, result in smaller plants in these regions. When situated very close to, or above, the Arctic Circle, plants benefit from the Midnight Sun, with unbroken light around the clock in summer. The soil in Iceland is volcanic and fertile and trees such as *Populus*, willow and birch are used to break winds and shelter other plants.

Seasonal opportunities

Designing a garden in Scandinavia unleashes creativity, as gardens resonate with every season. Shoots in spring make us appreciate new life, and the fresh green of every summer is equally invigorating. In autumn we slow down as the light weakens, and the previously vivid colours grow cooler and quieter in winter. When working with gardens in Scandinavia, we live between hope and despair and constantly look to what is to come. It is hard to predict the weather, and seasons can appear different from one year to the next. Sometimes the winter comes early and we miss taking care of the last crops; some springs and summers are very dry and we must keep a close eye on the garden; while other summers are rainy.

Sheltered lounge area
—
On delightful summer evenings and chilly autumn afternoons alike, an outdoor fire can make a captivating feature in a space. By using a countersunk structure the connection to the garden becomes more intimate; it is viewed from a lower perspective. This countersunk area in a garden by John Robert Nilsson Arkitektkontor in Värmdö, Sweden, made from Norrvange limestone provides interesting views, at the same level as the pool and overlooking a panoramic view of the archipelago, while being sheltered from strong winds.

Everything living adapts over time, to survive, and cope with, the circumstances in a region. Plants that grow locally are used to the region. They know the seasons and are used to the relatively short summers, when many peak and are at their best. They are strong individuals, survivors, which give us their all when they burst out in bloom, only to later retract and prepare for hibernation.

Planting through the seasons

Year-round interest is important in any garden, providing a constant uplifting feeling in the space beside the house. In a minimalist approach, planting could consist of few carefully selected species that undergo very little seasonal change, such as clipped hedges or grasses only. Alternatively, a garden can be planned with a range of plants that change with the season, with some playing a key role in spring, others in summer, and the rest in autumn and winter, allowing for more seasonal moods. The latter is more common, as many of us find variation exciting, with plants in bloom for as much of the season as possible. Some plants have a longer seasonal interest than others and these are useful to include for good continuation in a border. *Hemerocallis* 'Stella de Oro', *Clematis* 'Paul Farges' and *Geranium sanguineum* 'Apfelblüte' for example, are all in blossom for a long period. On the other hand, we also tend to have a fascination with plants with a very limited time in blossom, such as cherry trees. Although we might wish that the blooms would last longer, the dramatic mass effect and power of short-lived plant blooms can be hard to resist.

Fragile springs

Spring is a very important season to Scandinavians. Landscapes are reborn, with early spring plants showing the first signs of life returning. Spring requires patience, though, as gardens develop at their own tempo and shouldn't be pushed and plants stressed. People actively start to look for signs of life in gardens, such as the first courageous snowdrops in bloom, or a willow showing its beautiful catkins. The light lasts longer during the days and many wrap up and seek a sheltered spot in the garden, just to feel the warmth from the teasing sun, despite the still freezing cold air.

By March gardens are at their most vulnerable, with mild temperatures during the day, potentially shifting drastically to freezing cold nights. We keep our fingers crossed that the icy melting time, the transition from winter to early spring, won't be hard on the plants. The snow that once gave insulating protection is now melting and gardens are exposed. Some plants start activating their roots in search for water, which may be fatal. Some parts of the garden, especially evergreen plants, can be helped by protection, such as a cover of burlap, to allow them to rest for a bit longer. We do the best we can to help gardens at this time, but the rest is up to nature to decide and perhaps we should believe in a bit of magic. If we patiently wait, surely they will suddenly arise before us in all their spring splendour.

Eventually, the danger is over and a more pleasant spring arrives, in most parts during April and May. These are gardening months and winter is long forgotten. Spring is short and intense in Scandinavia; you can literally hear gardens bursting into life. Green shoots pop up like mushrooms, insects are wide awake, spiders work in their webs and ladybirds paraglide through the branches. Gardens change by the day and you have to be outside frequently to capture the growth and transformations. What once looked like a lifeless place is now lush and green.

Dark autumn contrasts
—
With gardens and landscapes full of yellow, amber and orange foliage, you may want to accentuate the fiery autumn show. A composition that includes dark foliage in a bright spot can look both seductive and luxurious when combined with yellows and oranges. The large flower heads of this lace-cap *Hydrangea macrophylla* 'Kardinal violet' held up by its golden foliage combine perfectly with *Actaea simplex* 'Brunette' and *Miscanthus sinensis* 'Nishidake' for a golden and deep autumnal border, seen here in Stockholm, Sweden.

Vibrant summers

The light has returned and temperatures rise. Summer in Scandinavia is vivid, almost to the point of absurdity. Everything is peaking, all at once, the sun refuses to set and plants are in full bloom. People spend more time outdoors than indoors, and by midsummer we almost live outside. Gardens grow vigorously, faster than we know, and for anyone interested in a free workout there is weeding to be done. Summer is when we use our gardens the most. We dine and entertain there, we eat breakfast and have barbecues outside, we play and we relax. In recent years outdoor kitchens and ovens have made an entry into Scandinavian gardens. They have not only become popular as a result of how much time we spend outside, but also provide a reason to stretch out the summer. At this time indoor tasks are far down the list of priorities, and gardens truly show their strength and vitality, peaking with the summer solstice, the longest day and shortest night of the year, which is around the time when midsummer is celebrated. The Sun never sets in the Scandinavian regions above the Arctic Circle, and the enthusiastic gardener can carry out work around the clock!

July is a delightful month, when relaxation in the garden might be at its height. The winds are mild, mornings start early, evenings last long and the water is pleasant. Many of us like to be close to water – lakes or barren cliffs, or sandy beaches by the sea. Outdoor swimming pools, popular with children and adults alike, can be seen in gardens in both the north and the south. By August we have entered the harvest season. Hopefully, with a good summer, all the hard work with the vegetable plot will have paid off, and we feel rested, with energy reserves to take us through winter. We try to prolong the summer evenings as much as we can, by still eating and entertaining outside. The light is softer with gradients of pink and the scents in a garden are noticeably enticing, especially in the evenings. Night temperatures are lower, with mist and morning dew. A new chapter is approaching.

Fiery autumns

Scandinavian autumn gardens can display fiery colours and truly divine landscapes. September is a great month for planting and carrying out maintenance work, with less heat and more moisture. It is refreshing to be outside on sunny days with crisp air and clear blue skies. Colours on the ground contrasting with the blue skies can be extraordinarily rich. We like to get cosy, and wrap up in blankets around outdoor fires. Adding light and warmth to the garden extends the enjoyment of being outside and outdoor fire pits – built-in, countersunk or freestanding – are sought-after spots in the autumn.

Gradually, rainy days and stronger winds roll in, making leaves fall like confetti to the ground. Yet again, the souls of Scandinavians change and we must confront mortality. Distant memories of flowering plants provide small sculptures in the garden, with a network of seed heads left behind; fading gardens show these beautiful features that are not prominent in summer. Seed heads and dead plumes alike are every bit as attractive as a blooming flower head, though they can be overlooked in their neutral costumes. Gardens containing many perennials may look less tidy at this time, but these plants also give spirit and character to the space, and at the same time providing shelter for wildlife. It is time to prepare for winter. The days are noticeably shorter and the temperatures lower in October, and in some parts further north the snow has already made an appearance.

Fabulous autumn berries
—
Euonymus europaeus
is a jewel, lighting up an
autumn garden even on
a gloomy autumn day,
as here in Stockholm,
Sweden. The shrub is full
of clusters of orange fruits
held by four split-open
magenta-coloured lobes.
As much as it provides
ornamental value,
looking remarkable and
exotic, it carries the bright
colour for a reason: a
warning that the fruits
are toxic.

Solemn winters

Life in the garden has had to beat a retreat.
Gardens are calmly quiet, and both people
and plants are in hibernation. Gardens in
southern parts may still look autumnal if
the winter is mild and the snow hasn't
fallen. Further north, however, it is highly
likely that snow has arrived in October
and November. The first nights of frosts
bring winter gardens to life, dressed in
shining crystals in all their glory. Structures
are startling and frameworks of branches,
along with evergreen plants, shape the
body of the garden. This is a good time to
plan for new projects in the garden, as it
is easy to get an understanding of the
strengths and weaknesses of the space
when studying it in its bare condition.
Successful winter gardens, providing
interest through structure and planting,
are very sculptural. Snow enhances
patterns in hard landscaping, such as a
wider grout in paving. Heavier snow gives
additional height to every flat surface.

If there is too much snow, though, we
may need to shake it off branches to
keep them from breaking. Naked trees,
stretching out bare arms, sometimes
dressed in interesting bark – such as
Prunus serrula and *Acer griseum* – act as
powerful focal points in gardens. Grasses
with plumes gently sway in the winds as
if it were summer. Most plants are at rest,
though, and so is the wildlife, protected
and hidden under layers of insulating
snow. They are all going to make it; they
are survivors.

Earliest spring flowers
—
Below: Plants early in the season are important and much appreciated in Scandinavia, as we have been waiting for them for such long time over winter. Snowdrops are among the first plants to show. Bulbs are rather quick-flowering plants, and you may want to plan them to come out in sequence, to enable enjoyment for a longer time. A good way to use them is to plants bulbs among foliage which is evergreen or appears early in the season, such as *Heuchera* or *Hosta*, hiding the often tired-looking foliage of bulbs just after they bloom, as in this garden by Zetterman Garden Design in Saltsjöbaden, Sweden.

Flowering across the seasons
—
Right: Diverse planting across the seasons is important. With less wildlife, our gardens and landscape would be dramatically diminished. Bees play an essential part in pollination, and without them we would not be able to pick apples in our gardens or blueberries in our forests. We can encourage them by planning soft landscaping with seasonal blooms, as wildlife has diverse needs. *Allium* is a bulb loved by honeybees, perfect to include in a scheme for spring and early summer interest, and also providing strong architectural lines, as seen here in Stockholm, Sweden.

Deferring to the surroundings
—
Scandinavia is a vast region rich in natural landscape variation, allowing for an array of interesting gardens. This rather small garden by ARKÍS arkitektar, is set in magnificent and majestic surroundings in Vatnajokulsthjodgardur, Iceland. By toning down the garden itself, it exudes character, and uses materials intended to be as neutral and natural as possible, deferring to the surrounding environment. A simple, strict and robust expression in the design provides contrast with the organic moss-covered landscape, yet naturally connects to the landscape through its colour, pattern and material.

Echoing cliff formations
—
Every garden has its
own unique starting
point. In this garden by
Jarmund/Vigsnæs AS
Arkitekter MNAL in
Vestfold, Norway both
wall structures and steps
seamlessly blend into
the surrounding natural
cliff formations. This is
expressed in the material,
the organic shapes and
the colour range. For this
garden, bordering the sea,
selecting appropriate
materials was important,
as strong winds and
intense sun and salt
combined would put
constant pressure on
construction.

Making the most of summer

—

Left Summer is the time to enjoy the garden, with all the hard work and preparations behind you, as in this peaceful space by Zetterman Garden Design in Saltsjö Duvnäs, Sweden. July is the peak of summer, with temperatures reaching 20–25°C, sometimes more, but gardens are still fresh and green. In exposed areas further north temperatures are more likely to reach only around 15°C, but at times the Sun never sinks below the horizon.

Tranquil sophistication

—

Below On late summer evenings we might finish the day with a swim. When adding water to a garden, with swimming pools and larger bodies of water in particular, consider how they will blend with the rest of the garden and the wider surroundings. Swimming pools are large and relatively solid in colour, so choosing a tile, stone or liner that includes colours close to natural water bodies in the region will help the pool to blend in comfortably. This pool by Zetterman Garden Design in collaboration with Per Öberg Arkitekter in Saltsjöbaden, Sweden uses a mosaic containing greens and turquoises, conveying a feeling of tranquillity and sophistication, and rests peacefully in the space.

Beach aesthetic
—
This garden by Johan Sundberg Arkitektur in collaboration with Maria Arborgh, in Höllviken, Sweden, is on sandy soil, and imitates the nearby beaches, with cobbles scattered among the planting for a relaxed look. An intimate relationship with light, nature and plants was central to this house and garden concept. Danish brick is used for the façade, connecting with the sandy soil in colour. The sparse, low-level planting provides an interesting interweaving carpet of globe-shaped perennials and grasses in clusters, with a couple of colourful autumnal focal points displaying splashes of orange and red.

Brilliant berries
—
Varieties of *Berberis* are highly valued in a wildlife garden, as they provide food and shelter for birds. Although the thorns aren't so good for us, they protect nesting birds and carry red berries, dangling on the branches, lasting through winter. The flaming orange shades will brighten up any autumnal garden, as here in Åre, Sweden.

Autumn display
—

Opposite: Autumn is a season when we can appreciate incredibly bright and fascinating foliage colours in Scandinavia. Planning a garden with a variety of plants and foliage can provide amazing contrasts between them at this time, with foliage in an array of yellows, oranges, reds, purples, ochres and rusts. In this garden in Saltsjöbaden, Sweden by Zetterman Garden Design the black wooden frame marks the space, and watches every moment of the transition.

Autumn leaves
—

Fiery reds and golden yellows are commonly thought of in association with autumn gardens, and in a year without heavy rain and winds, the wonderful colours can last for many weeks in Scandinavia. Just like supercharged confetti falling to the ground, this *Prunus sargentii* spread its leaves on the garden floor in Stockholm, Sweden. Solid paths, however, might become slippery with wet leaves, so it is wise to keep areas with heavy traffic clearer.

A garden for all seasons
—

With a strict central axis, this sculpture garden by Paradehusets Tegnestue/ Paradehuset Landscape Design Studio, in Midwest Jutland, Denmark, is built up of giant raised beds with steel edging. The central bed is filled with spring bulbs and evergreen ground cover, while others are planted with a variety of perennial grasses mixed with perennials, reaching their visual climax from mid to late summer. The various plants work well in autumn too, with a more neutral colour spectrum. Lighting enhances the space during the darkest months of the year, adding to the experience from the inside the house.

Painterly composition
—

Below Making borders wide gives the option for more creativity with plant combinations. This very generous space in a garden in Sealand, Denmark by Tidens Stauder Design allows for working with plants as an artist would paint a picture. It shows how much colour, texture and shape can be left in a garden, even with hardly any flowers in bloom. The tree, *Prunus avium*, is central to the space, providing a dramatic change in height and scale.

Summer rain
—

Right Summers in Scandinavia are subject to sudden changes. Some days or weeks are sunny and pleasantly warm, without many clouds in the sky. Others are full of surprises, with mornings very still and silent, later giving way to heavy rain, thunder and lightning, with clear blue skies to follow, and perhaps, with a final rainbow as a reward. Rain in summer makes gardens feel very fresh, with scents enhanced by the moisture. The sunbeams hitting raindrops on plants and foliage like this *Briza media*, seen in Stockholm, Sweden, make them appear even more graceful.

Purple splendour
—
Early morning in late October and the mornings are noticeably darker, especially in the very north of Scandinavia. Further south we are still lucky enough to enjoy the daylight for a bit longer. Gardens that had vivid autumn colour have now lost their intensity and seem turned down. *Atriplex hortensis* 'Purpurea' stands tall and quiet in this garden by Tidens Stauder Design in Sealand, Denmark, carrying its seed heads alongside the dark silhouette of *Eupatorium maculatum* 'Album'.

Autumn mysticism
—
Even on the duskiest
of days, a late autumn
garden can have the most
fascinating expressions
and mystical moods.
Long and tall structures
give perspective to this
space by Tidens Stauder
Design in Sealand,
Denmark. *Sedum*
'Herbstfreude' shows the
reason for its nickname,
'Autumn Joy' in this
garden, tethering the
pergola firmly to the
ground with its dark
and dense foliage, while
the *Phuopsis stylosa*
'Purpurea' comfortably
rests in sweeping gestures
along the gravel path.

Spectacular foliage
—

Opposite: All plants have their highlights, and how plants are arranged in a space will have an impact on how noticeable they are. Many trees carry eye-catching foliage, such as *Acer palmatum*, *Quercus palustris* and *Cercidiphyllum japonicum*. Looking closely at the ornamental *Cercidiphyllum japonicum*, seen here in Stockholm, Sweden, colours mark every vein in the leaf and stalks are vividly pink. Nature provides us with incredible resources to use in our gardens, if we look for them.

Time to work
—

Autumn can be very pleasant in Scandinavia, with clear blue skies, fresh air, and with winds still mild and temperatures pleasant. It is a great time to carry out gardening work, and any fixing that needs doing. Baskets, wheelbarrows crates and other garden tools come in handy, made easier to use when kept in one place, as in this space by Paradehusets Tegnestue/Paradehuset Landscape Design Studio in Gisselfeld Kloster, Denmark.

Seed pod display
—

Some plants reach their visual peak with their seed pods, and not their flowers. *Physalis alkekengi*, commonly called Chinese lantern, appears very quietly in summer and the white flowers can be hard to spot. Later in the season, however, it grabs all the attention with its highly attractive orange seed pods providing ornamental value in an autumn garden, as here in Stockholm, Sweden. They are ideal to bring inside and use for decoration, as they keep their colour when dried.

Autumn dawn

—

Early morning light in
late September, when
the garden is still asleep,
the dawn whispers
gently in this garden by
Tidens Stauder Design
in Sealand, Denmark.
The moisture in the air
decorates the foliage,
and grasses hold water
drops like jewels in a
crown. Silence is golden,
and the only sound that
can be heard is the
crunching of the gravel
if anyone approaches.
The *Clematis montana*
drapes over its throne in
the rear, perhaps sensing
summer is over.

Late-flowering loner
—
Sometimes an autumn plant stands alone in its glory; a curious loner in the garden, observing how the rest of the plants have already started to prepare for winter. The dark and golden-yellow *Rudbeckia fulgida* var. *sullivantii* 'Goldsturm' is a late-flowering perennial, boosting a garden with a last lick of colour, and bringing happiness and enthusiasm to an autumn border, as here in Stockholm, Sweden.

With dramatic seasonal variations, changes can happen unexpectedly in our gardens. Despite this, the first frost is always spellbinding, putting a different mood on a garden: inviting, yet sculptural, and as if the flowers might break if we touch them. It is easy to see why Scandinavia is perceived as being pale and cool, especially at this time of year, as shown in this garden in Sealand, Denmark, by Tidens Stauder Design.

Winter drama
—

Above: January is a time
of new beginnings. Only
a few weeks earlier the
sun would not reach
above the horizon in the
very north of Scandinavia,
and everyone is grateful
for each new day with
daylight stretching a little
further. Gardens can look
striking at this time of
year, such as this garden
in Sealand, Denmark by
Tidens Stauder Design
with its artistic
composition of hedges.
The taller, light ochre
Fagus frames the space,
while the dark green
Taxus has been clipped as
a set of stairs, enclosing
low *Buxus* close to the
ground. Round spheres
placed in straight rows
seem as if they might be
guarding a treasure.

Sculptural shapes
—

Right: This garden
by Zetterman Garden
Design in Saltsjö Duvnäs,
Sweden has a similar
character in winter and
summer, having been
created with strict shapes
and evergreen planting.
Although it does not
change much with the
seasons, its sculptural
nature comes into its
own in winter. A large
feature jar is placed in
one of the squares, and
is illuminated in the
evenings, enhancing
its bold shape.

Bark and snow
—

Trees, apart from their vertical interest, give body and shape to a winter garden, with each tree having a unique silhouette. Attractive bark also adds interest, through its colour and texture, for example *Betula albosinensis* var. *septentrionalis*, *Stewartia pseudocamellia* and *Betula utilis* var. *jacquemontii*. This ornamental multi-stemmed *Acer griseum* is a gem in a garden – as here in Vallentuna, Sweden, by Zetterman Garden Design – covered in snow, with its shiny, peeling copper bark.

Left: With pleasant summers, a swimming pool with a nearby eating and entertaining area is much used in this garden.

Opposite, above: The front garden shows a pronounced architectural expression in winter, as well as during summer, with spherical evergreen shrubs and multi-stemmed trees.

Opposite, below: With autumn approaching and the light very low, interesting shadows and strips of natural light give depth to the space.

Plant list (selected)
—
Euonymus 'Sarcoxie'

Euonymus fortunei
'Emerald Gaiety' Dafo

Buxus sempervirens

Pinus mugo var. *pumilio*

*Sempervivum
arachnoideum*

Sempervivum tectorum

Cerastium tomentosum

Acer pensylvanicum fk.
Västeråker E

*Cercidiphyllum
japonicum* fk. Göteborg E

Carpinus betulus

Year-round strength and continuity in Sweden
—

Saltsjö Duvnäs, Sweden
Design by: Zetterman Garden Design
880m²

Scandinavians are so used to seasonal changes that for many, it is not a 'real' winter without snow, or an autumn without vivid colours. For this client, however, the desire for a garden that would be visually interesting and architecturally strong all year round took priority over accommodating seasonal changes. Moreover, the client wanted a garden that required an absolute minimum of maintenance throughout the year, without a lawn, but focusing on comfortable areas for relaxation and socializing, and including a swimming pool.

The design process started with a strong outline in terms of shapes,

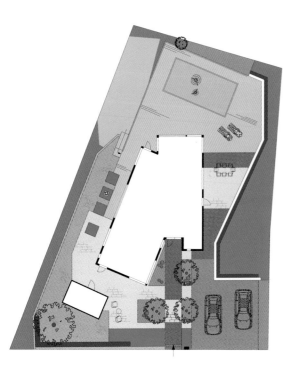

borrowing dimensions and directions from the house. Using the width of the front door as a starting point made a clear and straightforward entrance leading up to the house. This enabled further work on arranging the given space into a pattern using squares and rectangular shapes, planned proportionally, to work as paths, entertaining areas or planting areas.

Plants were selected for the garden that would look orderly and tidy at all times. The stiff square shapes help the eye perceive the garden as orderly even if a single planting doesn't necessarily look impeccable. The green plants have been selected to vary in height, giving dynamics to the space. To compensate for the missing green element of a lawn and to balance the formal part of the garden, a large wildlife meadow was implemented: bursting with life in summer, and a true haven for bees and butterflies, while remaining maintenance free all summer, when the garden is designed to look as stunning as at other times of the year.

As autumn approaches, some of the foliage in the garden stays green while hedges and trees turn bright yellow, just as in the nearby surroundings. The *Cercidiphyllum japonicum* fk. *Göteborg E* provides a rainbow of colour in each leaf, forming a true focal point in a corner. Lighting starts to become noticeable and useful at this time, both in the garden and on the façade of the house, with various fittings throughout the space.

In winter the main colours in the garden are green and white: evergreen foliage covered in snow. A large feature jar in the garden and various sculptural bollards are more prominent at this time of year. The garden is at rest, yet looking polished and cared for, and needs no more attention than snow shovelling when necessary.

Left: The summer palette of vibrant pure green turns to striking fiery colours in autumn: yellows, purples and oranges.

Opposite, above: A retaining wall and hedging combine to gently enclose the dining area, providing privacy and a fresh green sensation in summer, with the sound and fresh smells of a meadow bursting with wildlife just behind.

Opposite, below: Planters made of slate, containing *Buxus* and pine, remain a constant presence through the changing seasons.

BOLD

Urban and environmentally friendly gardens

If things are new, we would like to try them. If things are innovative, we are curious to find out how they are done. Scandinavia is a region that embraces development. People are open-minded and interested, welcoming new ideas. But we are also selective in terms of what we approve of, and seek out high standards and exemplary results.

Scandinavia has a proud tradition of success in many design fields such as architecture, technology, product design and fashion. All the Nordic countries are ranked among the most innovative countries in the world; ice skates, the loudspeaker, the paper clip and the zip are all examples of Scandinavian ingenuity. In the world of gardens, the Swedish botanist Carl von Linné developed the systematic classification of plants, the Systema Naturae. Today we often look beyond our own boundaries for inspiration, keeping a close eye on the latest trends from around the world. We are a small region, but we are alert and don't want to miss opportunities. We tweak ideas to make them our own – with integrity, to suit our needs and to resonate with our ethos.

Looking forward

Modern gardens in Scandinavia are often calm and mellow, but there are also contemporary gardens that reflect a totally different side of the north, showing a resolute and powerful side. You could draw a parallel between these radical garden expressions and certain experimental fashions and confrontational music, or the darkness behind the passion for so-called 'Scandi crime' or 'Nordic noir' fiction. They are fearless and fierce. These gardens express themselves with bold structures, deep and energetic colours and strong contrasts, with the aim of creating an atmosphere that is at once dramatic and sophisticated, and sometimes extremely persuasive.

Such gardens may involve elements that have not been covered previously, and commonly include bespoke structures. When there is an open attitude and freedom to pursue artistic ideas, expressions can take shape with the use of materials in new ways or touches to a garden that veer away from the norm. Unlike a more conventional garden, these gardens tend to have fewer references to previous design work. Risky, you might say, but taking risks also means results can be triumphant.

Being innovative and daring in design isn't only about aesthetics. In the 21st century we are aware that caring for the environment is crucial, and this engagement is growing stronger by the hour, among individuals as well as in design fields – with garden design being no exception. We are devoted to helping our planet, by going back to basics and reducing the amount of resources put into our creations. Material choices are discussed. The use of reclaimed and recycled hard landscaping and untreated woods are explored, as well as the sourcing of local plants. We must continue to set good examples by our work, and take responsibility for every change to our environment, ensuring it contributes to a better world.

Environmental consciousness

Gardens are not a stand-alone topic, but are connected to other complex challenges that we currently face. In urban landscapes and large cities, in particular, we have reached a point in time where we have to start controlling the flow of resources, how we use waste water and work efficiently with energy and heating, and how we handle our waste. Just as in many other places around the world, ongoing projects are taking place in Scandinavia on a large scale – looking at how to make our world a greener, better place to live in. With cities growing in size and with environmental impact in focus, sustainable approaches are being explored, for example, developing living roofs. In dense cities, where space is critical and limited, making use of vertical space – so-called vertical farming – could

Framing and echoing
—
Framing the landscape seems to bring nature closer in this garden in Li, Finland, by Piha- ja vihersuunnittelu Villa Garden, connecting it with the surroundings. Using a bold wooden structure makes the green element clearly visible and focuses the eye on selected views and specimens, such as *Hydrangea paniculata* 'Mustila', *Thuja occidentalis* 'Brabant' and *Pinus sylvestris* in the garden and beyond. The dark amber colour of the frame is echoed in wooden pergola structures further away in the garden, as well as in the colour of the pine bark of the towering *Pinus sylvestris* in the forest.

be a future solution, and is currently being piloted. Growing edible plants in vertical spaces and using space efficiently in densely populated areas also helps to minimize the use of water and soil, while maximizing the use of restricted light.

Be water wise

Rather than implementing irrigation systems in the garden, plan the soft landscaping to cope with and thrive in the given conditions: you will save both money and water. In regions with temperatures that drop below zero, exposed pipes can break and lead to costly consequences – not only for the wallet, but also for root systems that get too wet, then freeze and die. If irrigation systems are used, you must shut them down properly before winter hits. Plants that are suited to the site will naturally grow stronger and healthier, and this helps conserve water. If the garden is dry and sunny, avoid creating an unnatural

habitat, but work with drought-tolerant plants instead, such as ornamental grasses, sedums and herbs. We are fortunate to have so many lakes and water sources in Scandinavia, naturally helping our horticulture and our gardens, and with a fair amount of rainfall in most parts, it is a good habit to collect rainwater. A water collector can be both functional and an aesthetically pleasing feature in the garden. Make it a habit to water plants in the evening, or when it is raining, to minimize loss of moisture through evaporation. In the old days, before today's rigid communal water systems, every farm had a decorative pump and well, and many of these can be seen in gardens still, though now mainly used as a feature rather than a functional object.

The value of old tools
—
Investing in durable tools made from wood and steel is a sensible approach in terms of sustainability, and also because they are a pleasure to use and feel authentic. For collecting water, you might want to consider using large barrels, which are durable and at the same time can look visually appealing. A collection of old watering cans provides a cheerful focal point in the garden, as in this space by Paradehusets Tegnestue/ Paradehuset Landscape Design Studio in Gisselfeld Kloster, Denmark.

Found objects
—

Arranged and designed gardens are never an exact replica of nature, but we do try to imitate the way nature works in places, and sometimes we come up with exciting ideas as a result of good fortune. This arrangement makes use of two objects found in this garden in Kalmar, Sweden, which could have been neglected, but instead become a charming feature in the space: an old granite trough and a pump no longer in use. Here they have been made into an attractive rural and simple water feature.

Only use organic matter

The strength and vitality of a plant depends on its root system, and many plants benefit from receiving additional nutrition in spring, when they start to grow and develop. By adding organic matter to the soil you can sustain the ecosystem in your garden, as the microorganisms will remain in the soil as well as help grow healthy, strong plants. Avoid chemical fertilizers, which are not retained in the soil but are instead transported into rivers, lakes and oceans, with negative consequences for the ecosystem. Incorporating and using a compost system will provide you with fine, nutritious organic matter, as seen in many gardens.

Weeds are considered our nemesis, but is it really a war worth fighting? Perhaps a few hours of weeding is a better solution than using chemicals, which can be harmful to people, pets, insects, plants and the soil. Not only do weed-killing

chemicals have a negative effect on our gardens, but they also flow into the water. Every now and then gardens might be hit by aphids or other pests, though. To guard against this threat, choosing the right plants and excellent soil is important. The healthier plants are, the less likely they are to succumb. Before finding a drastic solution if pests do take over, find out how bad the problem is and be sparing with chemicals and pesticides. In many instances the pest will disappear naturally after some time, or you can prevent it with natural and gentler methods, such as soap.

Buy quality, reuse, reclaim

With any product, buying good quality and getting into good maintenance habits will prolong its life. High-quality tools made of steel and wood rather than plastic will last for a lifetime, and perhaps longer. It can be convenient to rent tools that you don't use often, or exchange and borrow tools for specific tasks not frequently carried out. If you inherit a garden with existing plants and paving, always analyse the site. You may well find things that can be reused, or alternatively passed on to someone else. You might also find plants that are highly valuable, sometimes overgrown, but which can be divided and shared, or replanted to give pleasure somewhere else in the garden. Think about using reclaimed paving stones, too. Every time we put a new stone into the garden, whether natural or artificial, we use up more precious resources. With so much rock in the ground, blasting is common in many places when building new houses in Scandinavia, and making use of excess quantities of this stone for gardens is common. It is ideal to use for walls, as it looks very natural. Moreover, plan paved areas sensibly, considering how to prevent flooding and allow for drainage of heavy rains or melting snow in spring.

Technology and automation

Just as inside your house, gardens can benefit from the use of certain gadgets. Use them to ensure that lighting is efficiently used and only on when needed, and consider efficiency when warming up the swimming pool for the season. Timers are excellent for this purpose, minimizing the environmental impact of such systems. Robotic lawnmowers can come in handy, with some even keeping you posted with messages via a mobile phone app.

Eclectic compositions

Art in a garden is a way to allow for freedom of expression. It could take the form of a sculpture which has relationship with the garden, using a material or pattern found elsewhere, or it might be a piece completely unconnected, telling a story on its own. Placing random things in the space, such as old sets of tools,

Exploiting material properties
—
Originality often means taking a risk, but the materials and construction methods used in gardens have limits. When trying something that has not been done before, it is vital to use good craftsmanship and understand materials and how they work in order to ensure durability. In this garden by Zetterman Garden Design in Stockholm, Sweden a sculptural expression on a small scale fulfils the purpose of breaking up a tame pattern.

can also be viewed as art. It could just as well be any collection of items close to the heart, adding a personal touch. Although not seen in every garden in Scandinavia, such artistic expressions, using items from the past, can be found every now and then, and are valued for the memories they evoke.

Using items throughout the garden in a collaborative and elaborate way can add a sense of humour to the space and provide refreshing surprises in hidden corners. When placed repeatedly or in groups, they paint a picture, tell a story or become a kind of theatrical play in the space. Other gardens may contain only a few selected items, such as a wooden wagon wheel, an anchor or an old lantern, yet still have a human touch that suggests a story.

Rooftop gems

Roof gardens are like gleaming gems in a city; persuasive and seductive outdoor spaces situated high up above the ordinary. They are particularly enticing in urban environments, often tucked away yet authoritatively looking out over the city. Roof bars and restaurants on roofs are becoming increasingly popular in Scandinavian cities, right in the centre of things and yet, need to be sought out. When visiting one of these roofs, it is pleasing to spy living roofs scattered around like green handkerchiefs across the urban landscape.

Green roofs
A sod or turf roof is a traditional Scandinavian type of green roof which has been used for centuries. During the Viking period and the Middle Ages most roofs were sod roofs, and this remained the most common roof in many parts of Scandinavia until the late 19th century. Materials were easily accessible, and they were functional – with birch bark in the base to ensure the roof was waterproof, and sod on top which made them insulating and held the bark in place.

Today, however, green roofs are not built from bark, but still confer the same advantages on a house, both providing insulation and having a cooling effect, and they also contribute to biodiversity. They help insects and minibeasts of all kinds, including bumblebees, spiders, beetles, birds and butterflies. These naturalistic roofs can be seen not only on large-scale developments, but often on smaller buildings in private gardens, such as sheds, guest houses, saunas and carports. A house or a building with a green roof will subtly blend in with the garden and with the surroundings, and becomes less noticeable when compared with one with a conventional roof. When viewing these roofs from high above, in an elevated garden for example, they appear gently hidden in the landscape.

Roof gardens and terraces
Roof gardens and terraces add value to a city and its buildings, improving life for the inhabitants. For people in a city, who often lead a hectic lifestyle, a roof garden can become the perfect hideaway in which to unwind. Gardens in general require planning due to restrictions imposed by the climate, and roof gardens must cope with even tougher circumstances, necessitating even more planning. When successfully designed, however, they can be utilized for a long time in the season and offer amazing views of the skyline, as well as the magic skies of the north – always intriguing and mesmerizing.

Planning a roof garden
Roof gardens are by definition strictly limited in size. Furthermore they are often restricted in terms of load-bearing, and must be designed with lightweight materials. As always, with challenges come opportunities, and it may be that you come up with something refreshing and innovative when planning the space, perhaps by using vertical surfaces imaginatively to maximize the area.

Reaching out to the surroundings
—
Roof gardens and green roofs contribute to the reduction of pollution in cities, improving air quality. This urban terrace by Gullik Gulliksen Landscape Architects, in Oslo, Norway, faces a busy street at the front. However, it has the advantage of large trees at the back, offering a green oasis to anchor one side, and also to connect visually with the soft landscaping in the space, proving an even greener terrace for people to enjoy.

Just as you might borrow from the landscape in a large garden in the country, so you may find interesting details around a roof garden in nearby objects, to pick up on. The space can be unified by making use of existing textures and hard materials found in the interior as well as the exterior of the building, or the walls nearby. Arranging the space so that interesting views are emphasized, while less attractive ones are screened off, will make them connect to the space beyond.

Plants need to be planned for carefully, as they will be exposed. Pots and planters are unnatural growing environments for plants, and they lack the natural protection from the ground. Sometimes a sheltered corner can help protect from strong winds, but it may also become too hot.

In general, roof gardens should be planned to cope with both strong winds and intense sun, with durable construction and drought-tolerant plants. Interestingly, plants that we might consider typical in Scandinavia are great options for a roof: tough ornamental grasses such as *Sesleria* and *Miscanthus*, or conifers such as *Pinus parviflora* 'Shirobana' and *Pinus mugo* 'Mops'. *Sedum* and *sempervivum* as well as herbs and other edible plants

that thrive in the sun are also worth considering for a roof garden. Many of them don't require a lot of space or soil depth, or fertilizer. Hardy climbers are ideal for growing at height, with clematis among the best options in the far north, such as *Clematis* 'Riga' and *Clematis* 'Violet Purple' E survive while a wider selection thrive further south in the milder winters. Plants seem to ground a roof terrace and provide contrast and softness against the dominant hard materials found in a city, while the sounds of traffic and life below make a comfortable rumble in the background.

Material investment
—
Bold expressions over large areas will require a substantial amount of material. Here 30 tons of corten steel was utilized in this design by DesignHaver in Funen, Denmark, to make the solid, rusty panels. Alignment a nd communication between the panels was a general objective for the given space, creating coherency throughout.

*Creating volumes
with concrete*

—

Using cast in-situ
|concrete in a garden
has the advantage of
creating solid volumes
in any shape or form,
leaving large, seamless
surfaces without joints.
This garden by Zetterman
Garden Design in Saltsjö
Duvnäs, Sweden uses
a natural cement colour
and a smooth texture,
but in-situ concrete can
also be made dark or
light. The formwork
material, such as
weathered timber, can
create expressive patterns
in the surface. These
large, clean, resolute
surfaces complement the
architecture of the house.

*Simple forms enhance
chosen elements*
—
Strong, simple forms
can be used as a platform
and foundation,
enhancing other objects
and placing them in the
spotlight. In this scheme
by Zetterman Garden
Design in Saltsjöbaden,
Sweden the sweeping
recessed circle defines
the seating area, making
the surrounding planting
more pronounced and
the horse sculpture
prominent. By recessing
the circle, this part of
the garden is given a
dramatic flair, rather than
being left flat and tame.

Changing compositions
—
Using freestanding
items means that they
can be moved around to
make new compositions,
whenever and wherever
you wish. In this garden
by Paradehusets
Tegnestue/Paradehuset
Landscape Design Studio
in Gisselfeld Kloster,
Denmark, the gigantic
old fig tree in a tub
provides a wonderful
backdrop for a gathering
of antique and
semi-antique garden
items: copper vessels,
wrought-iron urns and a
marble basin. In winter
the fig tree is wheeled into
the barn for protection.

Articulation of space
—
Opposite: In this pergola
by Johan Sundberg
Arkitektur in collaboration
with Jessica Hallonsten
in Kämpinge, Sweden,
the lines are resolute,
the beams are sturdy
and the dark colour is
seductive. A structure
like this clearly makes
its voice heard and
gives authority to the
space. The pergola
marks out the enclosed
area underneath as if
it is guarding the tiles
on the floor. The floor's
pronounced patterns
contrasts with the rest
of the space, with
the concept of a
Mediterranean hideaway
within the garden.

*Art to enhance the
feeling of a space*
—

This garden by Piha-
ja vihersuunnittelu Villa
Garden in Li, Finland is
situated close to a river
and a dense forest, and
the aim was to relate
the space to both. This
sculpture was created
by a local artist, Sanna
Koivisto, and symbolizes
the embracing of the
day, the light and the
sun. This links to the
sunbeams that are
typically reflected in the
river, visible in particular
from where the figure
stands in the garden.

Games in the garden
—
A garden is a space where outdoor activities and hobbies can take place. A lawn is an area in which to play football, badminton or other outdoor games. This front garden by Green Idea in Oulu, Finland offers entertainment – at least for those interested in golf – with a putting green incorporated into the design. Including places to exercise and play can be pleasing to all: old and young alike. It can also encourage people to spend more time outdoors and to socialize in different ways in the garden.

Expressive materials
—
Opposite: Corten steel has a patina that protects it from corrosion, hence its suitability for outdoor compositions. Aesthetically it suggests an agrarian strength, connecting to the soil through its brown colour at the same time as it embodies structural strength, being used for detailing and bespoke larger units alike. In this garden by Zetterman Garden Design in Saltsjöbaden, Sweden, this corten steel tree sculpture by Atopia Art & Design forms an inviting focal point. Stripes of rust running down the concrete plinth connect it with the ground, like roots reaching for water.

Evolving design
—
Working actively with a design scheme to tweak it may result in new ideas – and if not, at least the opportunity has been explored. This atrium garden by Johan Sundberg Arkitektur in collaboration with Jessica Hallonsten in Kämpinge, Sweden balances a successful relationship between strict shapes in a collage of colour and materials. It acts as an enclosed room hidden from the surroundings, connecting with the house and the interior. The great white wall stretches out, linking with the swimming pool and continuing further into the garden, gradually bridging to green areas beyond.

Use what you find
—
Taking care of gardens and seeing what you learn and find fun may enable you to become an artist in your own garden. An eclectic collection of garden urns, pots and containers in various materials stands at the entrance to a narrow space in this garden by Paradehusets Tegnestue/Paradehuset Landscape Design Studio in Gisselfeld Kloster, Denmark, which is dominated by a free-flowing climbing *Hydrangea petiolaris* perched atop the garden wall.

Freedom of expression
—
By being curious the mind stays receptive to new ideas, which may open up a world of opportunities. Swimming pools were not seen in gardens in Scandinavia until recently, and now they are relatively common. With many gardens situated in sloping and steep terrain, making use of a dramatic drop can enable a daring expression, such as in this garden in Värmdö, Sweden by DAPstockholm in collaboration with Nod Combine – where the pool reveals an underwater window.

Creativity in a restricted space
—

Think of a space as your very own and you can find something to enjoy. This roof terrace in Stockholm, Sweden by Zetterman Garden Design is extremely long and narrow. Excitement was created by using structures to frame the view. *Parthenocissus* is used in the planters, to spread up the wood structures as a green curtain in summer, and provide rich dark red colours in autumn, corresponding to the colour of the door and window frames.

*Surroundings provide
design clues*
—
Just as with analysing the
space and surroundings
in a garden, making an
assessment of a roof
space can give clues to
concepts and details. The
colour scheme for this
terrace in Stockholm,
Sweden by Zetterman
Garden Design was
picked up in the black
slate flooring tiles and
roof panels, with bespoke
black seating to match.
The dusty pale yellow
colour of the wall is
reflected in the thinner
horizontals of the bespoke
bench and planter, with
the inverse of the black
stripes in the structure
for climbing plants.

Coherent concept
—

Opposite Working
through a concept
for the entire space is
important when planning
a garden; once it is in
place it may be difficult
to change. Corten steel
differs from the
alternatives of stone
and wood in its thickness
and its colour. The
panels in this garden
by DesignHaver in
Funen, Denmark are
large, yet they appear
light, because they are
very thin. The brown
conveys concepts of earth
and fertility, and its rich
warmth uniquely plays
with a flowering carpet
of yellow *Sedum sieboldii*
'Nana', *Hylotelephium
sieboldii* and *Sedum
spathulifolium*, making
the space confident
and vibrant.

Bold yet natural
—

Bold expressions
often work well when
juxtaposed with the
opposite. In this front
garden in Värmdö,
Sweden by DAPstockholm
in collaboration with
Nod Combine, the
hard-landscaped car
park structure made of
cast in-situ concrete
shows no signs of
compromise, but proudly
carries the wild grass
and the rampant natural
surroundings so that the
view from the house is of
a grassy wilderness rather
than cars. The light grey
solid colour makes it feel
motionless and safe.

Honest expression
—
The appearance of
steps is determined
by how the tread, riser
and nosing are treated.
This garden in Saltsjö
Duvnäs, Sweden by
Zetterman Garden
Design uses cast in-situ
concrete in retaining
walls to seamlessly
continue the riser of
the step, while the tread
is made of limestone.
The riser shows an
expressive and honest
contrast through the
exposed concrete, and
is aligned with the
limestone, not hidden
and set back by a nosing.

Evening extension
—
Summer evenings in Scandinavia can be comfortably warm. Ambient lighting on this roof terrace by Zetterman Garden Design in Stockholm, Sweden prolongs the evening and connects to the rooms inside, effectively extending the interior. Indirect light is used here, directed at tree canopies, and hidden in ornamental grasses, making the terrace interesting from the inside as well as out.

223

Integrated environmental design
—
Houses and gardens are not stand-alone entities, and with the complex environmental challenges that we are facing today this becomes even more evident. The house in this garden by Snøhetta, in Larvik, Norway, has a sloping roof surface clad with solar panels and collectors. Together with geothermal energy from energy wells in the ground, this serves the energy needs of the entire house (and generates enough surplus to power an electric car year-round). The outdoor swimming pool also utilizes solar-generated thermal heat surplus while the sauna is heated with firewood. Thermally treated ash planks have been carefully selected for the decking around the pool, and a visually interesting vegetable garden is incorporated into the scheme, containing herbs such as chives and mint, apple trees, and berry plants such as redcurrants and blueberries.

225

Working with the climate
—

Opposite: Great design can still care about the environment. This outdoor atrium in a scheme by Snøhetta in Larvik, Norway is a hidden gem in an area with a harsh climate, as it is sheltered from strong winds. It is made out of stacked firewood and brick and opens for outdoor dining from early spring to late autumn. The floor is made from slices of reclaimed railway sleepers, without any treatment.

Light, practical wood
—

Wood is a very practical material to use for terraces in Scandinavia, coping with our weather conditions, available in a range of dimensions and light in weight. This terrace by Gullik Gulliksen Landscape Architects in Oslo, Norway uses environmentally friendly heat-treated pine. Large planters allow for various planting options and help to protect the plants with a greater soil depth and more retained moisture. These planters, although large in size, are made lighter by using thin, spaced horizontals across each side.

Hardworking corner
—

Roof gardens and terraces are often limited in size, and planning is key to make them both functional and visually pleasing. Multifunctional items to save space and maximize storage are also useful. This space on a roof terrace in Oslo, Norway, by Gullik Gulliksen Landscape Architects, is created as an intimate corner for contemplation, but the choice of furniture also makes it an uplifting focal point with its joyful light yellow colour.

Plant list
—

Sedum sieboldii 'Nana'
Hylotelephium sieboldii
Sedum spathulifolium
Taxus baccata
Rodgersia podophylla
Imperata cylindrica
'Red Baron'
Amalanchier canadensis
Parrotia persica
Crataegus lavallei
Carex morrowii
variegata

Feature walls and coherent Danish expression
—

Funen, Denmark
Design by: DesignHaver
200m²

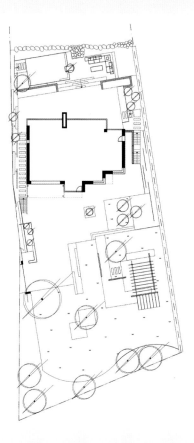

Design matters. Strong geometric lines, in both vertical and horizontal planes, can be used to lead the eye around a garden. This garden has been designed at a 10-degree angle to the property. By using the same angle in all areas of the garden, a coherent expression is achieved throughout the space. The angle breaks with the lines of the house, giving the perception of a garden that is dynamic and exciting, with interesting views and alignments as you walk through the different areas.

In this garden, close to the sea in Denmark, feature walls were central to the design scheme from the start, with the brief of creating a unique garden that included some unusual materials.

The proposed materials for the feature walls were granite or corten steel – two materials with distinct properties, requiring different construction methods, as well as being very different visually. The texture and colour of granite would seem less surprising in the garden, as it would resonate more closely with the environment, being a natural stone. Eventually, the decision was taken to work with the solid, brown corten steel for a bold expression. The balance of mass and void, of soft and hard landscaping, and colour all provided a particular spatial awareness: an understanding of how objects – including the occupants – are organized within the garden.

The large screens are used both in the front and rear garden, as well as on the side path, placed with care, linking the spaces. Leaving the semi-enclosed screens frames the greenery of the garden. Rather than the norm of green being used as a backdrop, here the corten steel frames enhance the foliage.

Planting has been carefully selected to contrast with the bold corten steel screening, and also to suit the coastal area, the mild climate and dry conditions, with two different and distinct characters in the garden. In the rear garden a more romantic touch is applied, using peonies and roses, while the front garden, close to the sea, contains plants such as ornamental grasses, cotton-wool grass and Japanese sedge grass.

Opposite: There is a strong aesthetic in both the front and the rear gardens. Corten screens complement lush green lawns, while a lounge area close to the sea uses colours that blend in with the nearby beach and the water beyond. Leaving the garden open towards the sea makes the lounge area connect to the surroundings and gives a sense of freedom to those using the space.

OPEN

A grow-your-own lifestyle close to nature

Scandinavians balance a hectic lifestyle with a desire to be close to nature. We are fortunate enough to have easy access to the wild, and exploit this when we need a break from the daily grind. We love and respect our land; it is a fundamental part of the Scandinavian soul. It is priority for many to escape the city at the weekend and in the summer months, and to spend time unwinding in a cottage tucked away in the wild.

Traditionally Scandinavians were farmers, with the vast majority of people living in rather modest, uncomplicated circumstances. To survive these primitive conditions our ancestors became expert gardeners, learning how to bring out the best in Mother Earth. To cultivate the soil is in our genes; this is what enabled us to survive. At the beginning of the 20th century the first allotments were created, used by city-dwellers to grow their own crops, while people living in the country also had their own small plot of land. Scandinavians have never lost their love of cultivating the land; either in a field in the country or in a private garden.

Dig in!

All gardeners have two things in common: they care about the soil, and they have an understanding of, and appreciation for, living things. Much about the way the natural world works can be understood through gardens; seeing the way living things work in symbiosis and are dependent on each other for survival. Gardening can educate and bring people and communities closer together – growing crops is fun and easy, and can more or less be done anywhere, in urban, suburban and rural areas.

Gardens in Scandinavia are relatively large and open, making them ideal for growing a smorgasbord of fruit and vegetables. With the current trends for being active and healthy eating, and an explosive development of new culinary experiences in the region, the use of domestic gardens for cultivation is reaching new heights.

Vegetables are turning tables

Scandinavian gastronomy has undergone a major transformation in recent years, moving beyond the cultural staples of salmon and meatballs, and it is not only the top restaurants that have taken food to a new level. Numerous restaurants in Scandinavia are today considered first class, and the use of local ingredients and seasonal produce is significant to this success. And it is not only the meat or fish that is regarded as the crown jewel of a meal, but vegetables too – and sometimes they are even more prominent. You can now visit restaurants that have rewritten the script; where vegetable dishes alone are served as a main course, with side orders of fish, meat or chicken as options. Some restaurants also produce their own herbs, or buy ingredients from nearby farms and growers.

Scandinavians often dine at home, and awareness of eating healthy food without preservatives or additives is much greater these days. Our culinary traditions have expanded considerably, and this has given rise to a new generation of gardeners with an interest in food.

Moving into the garden

The Scandinavian preference for outdoor living, combined with current food trends, influences the prominence of outdoor kitchen areas and kitchen gardens. It is a tradition in Scandinavia to invite friends and family to our homes, and although we eat out frequently, we also spend a lot of time at home. The way we live affects how we use our garden, and being able to cook in an outdoor kitchen, complete with pizza oven and built-in barbecue, is growing in popularity.

A well-designed outdoor kitchen enables you to cook beyond the summer season, too. When planning an outdoor kitchen, think about how it will be used, what food will be cooked, and how many the kitchen should cater for. Think of the practicalities of carrying food, plates and cutlery, and whether appliances should be stored in the outdoor kitchen. Just like everything else in the garden, the kitchen will need to withstand the prevailing weather conditions, and materials should be selected accordingly. Consider both function and aesthetics; for example,

Sculptural supports
—
Beans and peas are fast-growing crops and, as with tomatoes and other crops that grow tall, support such as a bamboo trellis or a steel mesh comes in handy, as in this garden in Forsby, Finland. You may want to plan your vegetable plot using bespoke tall structures such as pyramid-shaped or cylindrical supports, which also act as sculptural elements in the space.

perhaps a roof is needed for extra protection, and making use of levels in the landscape will work as a backdrop. A freestanding kitchen can act as a spectacular focal point, integrated into the landscape of a large garden as a place around which to socialize.

Growing trends

Innovation, new concepts of cooking and new ways of using what might once have been considered dull vegetables and berries have contributed to a renewed interest in growing edible plants. How much time we want to spend gardening, though, as an absorbing hobby, or just for the fun of casually harvesting a handful of herbs and berries, is a personal choice. With grocery stores offering an abundance of fresh food these days, most people can afford to be selective in what they grow, bearing in mind that their time is limited. Still, there is often a desire to grow a few

edibles in the garden. Those who are more committed may be willing to adapt their lifestyle to become self-sufficient, dedicated to growing as many edible plants as they possibly can, and eating their own vegetables throughout the year. Whatever your disposition, serving home-grown vegetables for dinner will always impress, and this can be done in any part of Scandinavia.

For the keen gardener there is a wide range of vegetables to choose from to grow, including tomatoes, cucumbers, carrots, beans, pumpkins, peppers, lettuces, beetroot, courgettes, asparagus, spinach, peas and radishes. New varieties appear every year alongside old ones with proven qualities for growing successfully. Growing fruit and vegetables in the Scandinavian climate does require some preparation. Due to the short season, it can be advisable to buy pre-grown plants, to give them as much growing time as possible in your garden. Generally

Multi-purpose garden
—
For this garden by Paradehusets Tegnestue/ Paradehuset Landscape Design Studio in Midwest Jutland, Denmark the aim was to create an old-fashioned working garden in a modern context. This space is designed to accommodate edible and ornamental plants together, with symmetrical plots for herbs and vegetables, and room for seasonal cut flowers. Strips of paving stones line pathways and separate gravel from cultivated beds. Robust iron frameworks support berry bushes, and espaliered apple trees add stability, while a small greenhouse houses seedlings early in the season, to get more out of the crops during summer.

speaking it is easy to grow vegetables, but they do need looking after – and just as in times gone by, a good harvest can never be taken for granted, with frost sometimes hitting unexpectedly in spring or even early summer.

Classics with cultural heritage

Salmon and meatballs aside, a plate of vegetables in Scandinavia in the past didn't look nearly as colourful as it does today. Fresh vegetables were few and far between, and only available in summer. Many had not yet been introduced to Scandinavia, and crops were grown mainly for survival, focusing on vegetables that could last over the winter such as onion, kale and parsnip.

It may not be something you think about much, but many of the fruit and vegetables that you chose to grow in your garden come with their own heritage and culture. For example, the important plants that were so useful that they enabled our ancestors to settle and survive, with the most significant in Scandinavia being the potato. With such a rich agrarian background there are plenty of edible species that hold high cultural value in Scandinavia: apples, pears, plums and cherries, to name a few. There is ongoing work in Scandinavia to maintain produce of such culturally important plants, and to preserve biodiversity. It is important to continue to grow these varieties, as they have proven to be resistant and most suited to our region.

Root vegetables

Looking rather muddy and dull, growing buried under the soil, root vegetables have sometimes been overlooked for fresh greens, but fortunately they have experienced a tremendous upswing in popularity lately, viewed as hip and almost exclusive, and sometimes used as a substitute for, or complement to, potatoes. Root vegetables have valuable nutritional qualities, and are often classed as so-called superfoods. Once washed and

worked on they are aesthetically pleasing, with their varied shapes and colours.

Beetroot, a vegetable at the top of the charts with its excellent nutritional qualities is highly popular – the conventional red kind, as well as the golden and the striped Chioggia beet. Beetroot is easy to grow, and thrives in most soils. It makes for great colour combinations on a plate or in a vivid soup – or a healthy drink for that matter.

Kale used to be far down the list of a desirable vegetable, but is now making up for years of neglect, as green kale contains an abundance of vitamins and minerals. It is versatile, being used in stews, soups, salads, drinks and even as crisps. Kale is a good example of a vegetable that also serves an aesthetic purpose in the garden. It is an architectural plant which, when mixed in with other varieties and less prominent plants, makes for interesting design compositions.

Berries

Plenty of delicious berries can be found growing wild in Scandinavia at the height of summer, which is all the more appealing as the freedom to roam and the right of public access allows anyone to pick berries for free. Blackberries prefer a mild climate and dry and sunny spots, and are often found in the maritime climate of southern Scandinavia: in Denmark, southern Sweden and along the coast of Norway. Blueberries become large and juicy in moist soil and partially shaded areas, and prefer a situation in deep forests, but can be found in many other parts as well, and in all countries of Scandinavia. If red lingonberries are what you're looking for, the best places to find them are among pine trees, where they thrive in acidic, dry soils, while golden cloudberries require moisture and are found in boggy areas, mainly in Finland, Norway and Sweden. In previous generations, berries were picked and stored to use as a source of vitamins during the long winter months. Today, berries are not critical as a source of vitamins in winter, but are sought more for the fun of picking and to provide an excuse for a nice stroll in the outdoors.

There are numerous berry varieties that will happily thrive in a garden, with classics in Scandinavia being raspberries, gooseberries and currants. Moreover, with the superfood trend, there is also an increase in the cultivation of unconventional varieties that are known to be nutritious and have specific qualities, such as trace elements and vitamins. Among these are sea buckthorn and black raspberry, breaking new ground.

Potatoes

Growing potatoes in Scandinavia is something of a passion. The potato has been used in Scandinavia for centuries, and the early varieties are ready to harvest by midsummer and are seen as a true delicacy. From midsummer onwards they can be harvested until autumn,

depending on the variety. There are numerous varieties to choose from, with some that go under a different name in each of the Scandinavian countries, such as a potato called *Rauðar íslenskar* in Iceland and *Gammal svensk röd* in Sweden. Some names are a bit humorous, such as the *Lange Svensk*, or the long Swede, grown in Norway. All types of potato are versatile and they tend to be eaten on a daily basis in Scandinavia. They can be stored for a very long time, over the whole winter, which accounts for their ubiquity. Potatoes are easy to grow, thriving in most soils, and are therefore a good choice for new gardeners. In the city they can even be planted in a large pot if a balcony is the only option.

Apples

At a farm in central Sweden stands a particular apple tree. This tree, Åkerö, is more than 200 years old, probably the oldest fruit tree of its kind alive today.

Array of apple varieties
—
Fruit and vegetables can be a feast to our eyes as well as our taste buds, and by planning an edible garden taking into account the seasons, the harvest will give you – and various wildlife – a varied diet, which we all need. By selecting early, mid, and late seasonal varieties you can get the best out of a plot. This installation by Emma Karp Lundström in Kivik, Sweden shows the wide range of colours that different apple varieties display, and is part of an artwork portraying flowers and bees called *Bee Nice*.

Thriving exotics
—

An 'exotic' plant is a non-native plant that has been introduced by humans, rather than spread to the region by itself. This kiwi plant, in Öland, Sweden, certainly sits at the more unusual end of the spectrum in Scandinavia. Planted beside a dark red, warm and sheltered timber house, these attractive fruits seem to grow quite large and juicy. Kiwi is very vulnerable to frost, however, so is only worth trying in the most southerly parts of Scandinavia.

From this tree, all other Åkerö trees in Sweden are descended, and this reflects how culturally important a plant can be. Apples date far back in history in Scandinavia, and mature trees can be found in many gardens. Apples, cherries, raspberries and various other berries are all examples of fruits that have been grown in the wild in Scandinavia for a long time, evidently doing well in the climate. Growers today work hard to maximize the produce, as locally grown apples are now sought after all year around.

Fruit trees, apples in particular, have never fallen from popularity in Scandinavia, and are as commonly incorporated into a garden today as ever. (As we all know, an apple a day keeps the doctor away!) The canopy of an apple tree requires space but provides a beautiful parasol for the garden if planted in the right place. Apple trees trained against a wall, or column trees,

are ideal for small gardens, and they also produce a crop that is easy to reach. With so many varieties available, you could grow enough apples to use all year, as long the frost doesn't take the flowers in spring or render it too cold for bees to pollinate the trees. Again, nothing can be taken for granted in our gardens.

Growing edible plants and enjoying them at their best is always something of a lottery in Scandinavia. Apart from the danger of frost early in the year, we need just the right amount of rain, and the right amount of sun and warmth during summer. Some years gardens totally explode with fruit with so much produce it is difficult to know what to do with it all – which, again, forms part of our psyche. Not only is fruit shared with friends and neighbours, but some is also taken to a local apple farm to produce apple juice. Today there are also dedicated websites used as billboards for anyone offering apples for free – anything to ensure nothing goes to waste, and to make the most of what we have.

Our celebration of the seasons is also evident through the produce we grow. Along with growing our own apples, various art installations and seasonal events take place in Scandinavia, where knowledge about our local produce and heritage is spread.

Strawberries

Strawberries are rather late arrivals to Scandinavia, first entering the north during the 18th century, yet now among the most popular berries to grow. At the end of June locally grown strawberries are treasured in Scandinavia, considered a highlight for many during midsummer. When the red berries burst into colour and sweetness, it is like a milestone heralding the start of summer. Wild strawberries, growing in the fields and woods as well as in gardens, hold a special place in children's hearts; they like to pick them to thread on stems of grass. As with most things that grow in Scandinavia, the season is short and intense. However, some varieties, such as 'Selva' and 'Rapella', flower and give fruit twice in the season. Strawberries are easy to grow, as long as they get enough water and sun, with early, mid-season and late varieties: 'Korona', 'Zephyr' and 'Bounty' are all common. They are a delight when consumed fresh from the bush. Alternatively they can be used to make jams or frozen to be enjoyed all winter.

Exotics

Gardeners are often curious souls. In Scandinavia you can choose to grow many indigenous vegetables and fruits, and failure is less likely to occur. For many keen gardeners, however, trying something new – perhaps a bit more challenging and daring – is looked upon with excitement. Part of the amusement factor in Scandinavia is that you may actually be surprised by what can grow. Sometimes plants follow growth patterns exactly by the book. Other times plants

that should thrive don't, while other plants – which in theory should not be suitable – do just fine.

For many of us, gardeners or not, there is a fondness and affection for the exotic plants we rarely see. Although mainly found in the south, in Denmark and southern Sweden, fruit such as quinces, peaches, apricots, figs, mulberries and grapes can be spotted, brought by the monks from southern territories centuries ago. Certain varieties of grapes can be planted for a harvest of sweet fruits, while olive and citrus trees are planted in pots, so they can be stored elsewhere in winter, away from frost and snow. Less-common plants like these often require more attention and care, but this has never stopped the true enthusiasts.

*The pleasure of a
potato harvest*
—

Opposite: The potato
is an integral part of
Scandinavian heritage:
it's what kept us alive
through the centuries.
Today this rough and
ready crop has morphed
from survival food to
delicacy. They come in
many different shapes
and colours: from the
purple spotted 'Blue Belle'
and the large, buttery
'Maris Bard', to petite,
pink salad potatoes like
'Cherie' and 'Amandine'.
To Elin Unnes, who looks
after an allotment in
Stockholm, Sweden,
growing these humble
tubers means
reconnecting with the
earth, physically as well
as metaphorically. Just
as you can't make an
omelette without breaking
some eggs, Elin believes
that it is impossible to
harvest your own potatoes
without returning home
dirtier and happier.

Timeless pursuit
—

Elin Unnes belongs to
a young generation of
gardeners, spending
much of her free time
at her allotment. In
Scandinavia many urban
gardeners keep small
allotments – even on
rooftops or in pots on
windowsills. To Elin the
word 'hip' – often used
in connection with the
current craze for growing
your own – is reductive,
overlooking the long
history of this practice.
It's not simply about
survival these days, but
is more about fun and
relaxation as well as
enabling creativity
and interaction with
the natural world: like
writing, or listening to
a great song.

Opposite The 'Victoria' plum is one of the most reliable and heavy cropping fruit trees, commonly seen in gardens in Scandinavia and also part of our fruit heritage. In early autumn, provided it's a good gardening year, the branches will sag under the weight of the sweet plums, and if you let your cooking creativity run wild the possibilities are endless: mouthwatering rum plum jams, slathered on to buttery toast or stirred into goat's milk yoghurt. Elin Unnes's top tips are 'drinking vinegars' – plums macerated in apple cider, vinegar and sugar; as well as sticky, spicy chutneys' and plum syrup reductions instead of maple syrup on pancakes.

Experimentation and risk
—

Edible plants such as vegetables and berries are design elements in a garden just as much as more obviously ornamental varieties. Every crop must earn its place, through superior taste and aesthetics: a hedge consisting of thornless blackberries, or a pot containing ornamental black 'Peruvian Purple' chillies. The new urban gardeners, who grow their own vegetables in order to feed their souls as much as their tummies, are not afraid to experiment,. The risk a gardener takes is part of the excitement, though not every experiment is a success, says Elin Unnes, of her allotment in Stockholm, but with every failure comes new knowledge. And hopefully at least a handful of crunchy black string beans.

Modern orangery

—

An orangery, on a base
of antique salvaged
Danish bricks, soaks
up the sunshine in this
spot, making it a perfect
place to incorporate the
exotics that we can't grow
outside in Scandinavia,
such as olives and citrus
trees. On the site of an
old barn, this part of the
garden by Paradehusets
Tegnestue/Paradehuset
Landscape Design Studio
in Midwest Jutland,
Denmark is restful and
ideal for growing both
edible and non-edible
plants. To accentuate the
space, a rustic fence of
chestnut branches weaves
its way through beds of
grasses and perennials
along the forest edge.

Versatile herbs

—

Left Plants, and herbs in particular, have been used throughout human history, in medicine and in food. Scandinavians particularly favour chives, parsley and dill, and these are commonly seen in herb gardens and used for all kinds of cooking. Herbs are excellent to grow as they require little space, and are suited to the city and the country alike, such as here in Forsby, Finland.

Bespoke vegetable planters

—

Below Many herbs and vegetables don't require deep soil, so larger pots and pallets can be suitable, and these are often seen in gardens. Some gardens in Scandinavia, however, sit on barren cliffs or slopes, and it can prove tricky to grow anything there. In these instances pockets between rocks are worth considering, or even bespoke planters that stand sturdily on a rocky slope, such as in this garden by Zetterman Garden Design in Lidingö, Sweden, where granite setts marry with the granite of the bedrock.

Unusual colour variations
—
Opposite Just as with ornamental plants, when it comes to edibles what we like is highly personal and subjective, with colour just as much a priority as flavour and texture. A tomato, for example – although usually red – comes in an array of colours and there is therefore scope to be creative, choosing green, yellow, orange or even darker colours. 'Indigo Rose', seen here in Uppsala, Sweden, is one of the darkest tomatoes, with an exceptional deep, dark red, almost black colour when exposed to direct sunlight. You might want to consider it when looking for bold and daring expressions in a vegetable garden.

Planning vegetable planting
—
Planning a vegetable patch such as this one in Julita, Sweden with as much care as an ornamental flower bed will provide visual interest to match the rest of the garden in summer. Starting early will enable you to explore the full range of varieties, some of which require preparation early in the year, before they can be moved outside. Planning a layout with care will allow form, texture and colour to interact, making the composition interesting and providing a valuable addition to the overall scheme of the garden.

Integrated kitchen
—

Plan and position an
outdoor kitchen with
care so that it blends
with the garden and
the wider surroundings.
You might want to
consider using a wall
or a natural cliff formation
as a backdrop, for
example. Alternatively,
you might plan the
kitchen to be freestanding
as a centrepiece in the
space. This garden by
Østengen & Bergo
Landskapsarkitekter,
in Oslo, Norway, has
panoramic views over
a fjord and catches the
evening sun, making it
an ideal place for wining
and dining. With hard
landscaping in Valz slate,
and the mix of materials
kept to a minimum,
the metallic kitchen is
seamlessly integrated
in one corner.

Saltsjöbaden, Sweden
—
In summer Scandinavians like to do everything outside. We hang out laundry, move our indoor plants outside, chill in hammocks and share meals. Outdoor kitchens, built-in barbecues, pizza ovens, fish smokers and other cooking facilities are increasingly a normal part of our gardens. This black beauty in a garden by Zetterman Garden Design in Saltsjöbaden, Sweden is made from Danish brick, fired to withstand the cold winters, with its chimney standing tall like a sculpture perched on a cliff. A sloping sedum roof gives character to the oven, matching a small herb garden that sits in a pocket of the rock just below.

Unobtrusive protection
—

With the summer season being relatively short in Scandinavia, a greenhouse within gardens makes perfect sense, preserving heat and allowing many crops to ripen faster. This garden in Li, Finland by Piha- ja vihersuunnittelu Villa Garden offers a simple and elegant greenhouse, making a statement with its frame, without screening off the beautiful nature nearby. In addition, crops are protected from any reindeer that may happen to take a stroll through the garden, munching on garden delicacies when you least expect it.

Linking with the forest
—

Forests are like large gardens that have to look after themselves; self-sustaining areas filled with diversity and a range of produce. Forests next to gardens, such as this one in Li, Finland by Piha- ja vihersuunnittelu Villa Garden share their depth and shades of green, injecting nourishing colours into the garden nearby, boosting motivation and creativity among the inhabitants. This garden connects to the forest through its planting and edible crops, featuring a greenhouse and berry-producing *Crataegus submollis* trees attractive to birds.

Design coherence across areas of a garden
—
There is scope to be creative, not only in terms of the choice of edible plants, but with the actual design of the kitchen garden or herb bed. As in this garden by Haver med stil, Have- og Landskabsarkitekt MMA in Østjylland, Denmark, it can be seamlessly integrated into the overall design scheme. This triangular herb bed sits in a sheltered corner with walls on each side. In other areas of the property identical forms can be found, but instead of herbs, these are filled with perennials and formal hedging. Therefore this design does not stand alone in the garden, but communicates with other areas that have different functions.

Potential of lettuce
—
Many vegetables are architecturally stunning. Growing lettuce is easy, and with the many possible texture and colour variations, there is scope to create the most bountiful artistic expressions in the beds. Lettuce requires moisture to grow well and develop a pleasant flavour. It is excellent to grow in Scandinavia as it doesn't require a lot of warmth. Large crispy heads can be mixed with loose, small varieties, such as *Lactuca sativa* var. *capitate, Eruca sativa* and *Lactuca sativa* var. *longifolia*, as here in Forsby, Finland.

Superberries
—
Opposite: Hippophae,
or sea buckthorn, is a
pioneer in Scandinavia,
and is a very common
shrub around
Ostrobothnia and
Åland in Finland,
where it has grown since
the last Ice Age. This
dazzling, spiny shrub
is most often seen in
coastal regions due to
its resistance to salt.
Sea buckthorn, such
as this plant in Kalmar,
Sweden, requires full
sunlight, but has very
few other requirements.
The bright orange
berries stand out in
an autumn garden,
looking slightly exotic.
The berries have become
immensely popular in
recent years, as they
are highly nutritious and
regarded as a 'superberry'.

Beautiful tomatoes
—
As well as tasting great,
tomatoes can lend artistic
flair to a garden. Their
spiralling stakes require
support, but they are
fun to grow, for adults
and children alike. The
tomato is a relative of
the potato, with many
cheerful and sometimes
slightly weird-looking
varieties to choose from.
The juicy red beauties
such as this wonderful
specimen, 'Trèfle du togo',
seen in Uppsala, Sweden,
thrive as long as they
get sun and shelter from
winds, perhaps in a pot
on a balcony in the city
or in a country garden.

Thanks to the soil
—

Below: Harvest celebrations take place all over Scandinavia, and make for the perfect day out in late summer. Crop demonstrations, information about new and old varieties, and various tastings are on the agenda. This artwork by Emma Karp Lundström, made from apples, highlights the importance of our soil. The artist raised the question of how we can better treat the soil and nature. This 108m^2 'painting' in Kivik, Sweden, called *Mother Earth*, is made from 35.000 apples including 'Katja', 'Cox's Orange Pippin', 'Red Gravenstein' and 'Alice'.

Urban rooftop farming
—

Right: With a greater awareness of sustainability, people increasingly have an appetite for urban farming. The dream of a little piece of farm in the city has come true at a rooftop in Østerbro, Denmark by ØsterGRO, Kristian Skaarup and Livia Urban Swart Haaland. Here the vision of making the city greener, focusing on organic food, richer taste experiences and local diversity, is a reality. Not only is it a green oasis in the city, but it is also a platform for teaching and sharing knowledge and inspiration.

Architectural artichokes
—

Strong architectural crops such as rhubarb and artichoke are popular with gardeners and gourmets alike. Artichoke can act as a striking focal point with its attractive appearance, creating visual interest in a mixed border as well as among other vegetables, such as here in Uppsala, Sweden. They may not be the easiest of plants to cultivate, requiring a long growing time and being sensitive to frost, but they are still the perfect choice for the keen gardener up for a challenge.

Biodynamic cultivation
—

More than ever before, we care about what we eat and what additives our food contains. Cultivating the soil in the most natural way, only using organic matter, helps both the ecosystem and individual plants to grow strong, as in these flower beds by Malin Skiöld. This garden in Stockholm, Sweden, Rosendals trädgård, uses biodynamic cultivation with a 'farm to fork' concept. Vegetables, herbs, flowers and fruit are harvested to use in the garden's café and wood-fired bakery. Biodynamic cultivation involves working with nature's cycles, in which vital pieces of the puzzle are composting, crop rotation and natural fertilizers.

Bee B&B
—
Bees are vital to the survival of a garden. They are pollinators to hundreds of species of plants, including fruit and vegetables. Some plants can pollinate themselves, but most require the help of a pollinator. You can help bees, and in the long run yourself, by using diverse planting in your schemes, with flowers in bloom at different times of the year. As a gesture of generosity – both for the fun of being creative, but also to help – you might want to offer them somewhere to stay in the garden during winter in the form of a 'bee hotel', as here, in Rönninge, Sweden.

Left: Construction
elements such as paving
and planters are situated
close to the house,
enabling the garden
further away to connect
with the unrestrained
and rampant forest.

Opposite: A lush green
lawn opens up the garden,
letting light into this
outside area as well as
into the house.

Plant list
—

Aronia prunifolia
'Viking'

Astilbe arendsii
'Fanal'

Astilbe arendsii
'Weisse Gloria'

Campanula carpatica
'White Clips'

Crataegus submollis

Festuca cinerea

Iris sibirica 'Shirley Pope'

Paeonia lactiflora
'Sarah Bernhardt'

Phalaris arundinacea
'Picta'

Populus tremula
'Erecta'

Ribes glandulosum

Salvia × sylvestris
'Mainacht'

Spiraea beauverdiana
'Lumikki'

Spiraea betulifolia

Spiraea japonica
'Odensala'

Syringa vulgaris

Thuja occidentalis
'Danica'

Thuja occidentalis
'Fastigiata'

Pinus mugo

Pinus sylvestris

Linking to the Finnish woodland
—

Oulu, Finland
Design by: Green Idea
1163m²

This garden is situated on the edge of a forest in Finland. To this young family it was important to retain the feeling of an open space yet not shelter it from the surrounding woodland. By working with conifers and utilizing natural rocks in the design scheme the garden allowed the woods to participate, yet not to intrude and overpower. Smaller decorative trees blend effortlessly with the mature backdrop and, due to their limited size, help to reduce the grand scale, making the garden seem welcoming and in proportion.

Apart from linking the garden to the surrounding nature, the aim was to create a garden in keeping with the architecture of the house, incorporating timeless, clean detailing. The creative opportunity comes from making use of the angles of the plot and the property in the scheme. By carefully mixing materials and patterns, and using strong angular lines, the layout of the space frames and enhances the house.

The front garden in particular relies on strong, angular components. The long straight lines draw the eye towards the entrance, making the area feel spacious and clean. Large planting areas are filled with natural irregular granite cobbles, reflecting with the surroundings. Columnar conifers provide height and balance as well as guidance towards the main entrance, just as symmetrical as the cone-shaped Finnish spruce in the forest.

The main outdoor entertaining area is kept open, facing sunny skies, with a terrace stretching along the side of the house and a generous lawn just below. The rear garden is kept simple. During the design process it became apparent that light grey and pearl blonde tones of the hard landscaping were important to balance the dark and black house, as well as creating contrast with the rich greenery of the lawn and nearby forest. The paving enhances the lawn with its interesting angular frame, also connecting with the house. Raised concrete planters flush with the terrace maintain the strict and orderly lines, yet also break up the space, filled with soft planting. Placing these planters close to the house was also an attempt to deter reindeer and other wildlife from eating the plants.

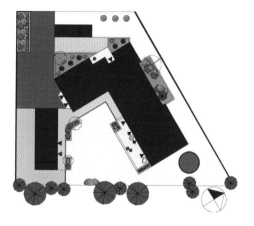

CARING

Stimulating spaces made for people to thrive

The Scandinavian countries are quite different from each other in some respects, but their way of life, the democratic view, their broadly similar languages (apart from Finland) and the approach to social welfare are some of aspects that lend this region a certain homogeneity. Their evolution in recent history – transforming Scandinavia surprisingly quickly from a region in which people lived mainly off the land, into a nation with sophisticated industrial societies – can be traced back in a large part to our access to natural resources: our water, woods and mines.

Scandinavians live in great freedom, in countries where people are regarded as the most valuable asset, with products and systems generally accessible to all. Scandinavian political systems, with ideologies of the state protection and redistribution of wealth to the people, started in the mid-20th century when a number of actions were taken to ensure equal access to education, healthcare, pension systems and insurance coverage, as well as maternity leave, among other initiatives. Scandinavia has some of the most generous roaming rights of anywhere in Europe. People and landscapes have always lived in symbiosis, and our gardens reflect this, encouraging activity, education and making us feel well.

Space to relax and recharge

All Scandinavian capitals – Copenhagen, Helsinki, Oslo, Reykjavík and Stockholm – are close to, or sit on, water. With more people moving closer to these growing capitals, they have to be accommodated. Many of these developments are waterfront housing and, by making use of deregulated spaces, new outdoor spaces are born. Many integrated landscapes today take this form, with the focus on liveable outdoor environments, bringing a mix of people close together. Landscapes are planned to encourage exercise, as well as integration and participation in the space. They are neutral places where everyone is welcome. The reality is that whether we live in a city, suburbia or in the country, many of us lead our daily life in the fast lane, wheels spinning fast, and this has resulted in a reaction: a collective longing for escape to simpler places free from stress.

A third space

Modern life often involves multitasking, with jammed schedules governing our everyday lives. We are surrounded by gadgets and devices to make us more efficient and keep us constantly updated. Weekend escapes may no longer be enough; we crave places close to us where we can unwind, such as a garden.

To use a quiet café or a library as a working space can be a refreshing change, and working from home can also be beneficial. Likewise a garden fulfils the promise of a space different from the norm – but unlike any other space, it is a stimulating environment which, through plants, light and life awakens our senses. To have your garden designed opens up possibilities for new activities, with areas to play and to socialize. Some gardens allow for additional houses, saunas and guest houses, and a smaller building might be used as an office space.

Beetles take over!
—
Unique playgrounds with a focus on artistic and architectural quality can be inspiring for both children and adults. In this nature-themed playground by MONSTRUM in Stockholm, Sweden, the creepy-crawlies are huge. The slightly dangerous-looking beetles are covered in beautiful patterns and colours, imitating real-life specimens, and children can climb around inside and on top. The playground is designed for children with disabilities as well, with wheelchair access to the large beetle and a ramp inside.

Not only do individuals reflect on how a garden can be used, but today many companies view their working environment as an echo of their values and who they are, which is why some in Scandinavia now offer a roof terrace or a courtyard space in which to work and relax. A corporate garden can be an inspiring space for employees to get energized, hold creative meetings or simply retreat for a break

Playgrounds

Children are naturally creative and can come up with the most imaginative stories, disappearing into another world when playing in a garden, regardless of how the space is arranged. Playgrounds as well as more natural spaces are important environments in which children develop. Playing outside gives them the opportunity to be creative, to learn how to interact with others, to take responsibility and to be educated.

Although playing is the priority for children, there is no reason why function must exclude aesthetic considerations in a playground. Just like gardens, they can be aesthetically pleasing and functional at the same time. When they become a part of the landscape, as a kind of sculpture or artwork, they are inviting for everyone – not only people intending to use the playground, but also for anyone passing by or overlooking the space. The rather fun and uplifting playgrounds shown in this chapter can be seen across Scandinavia, injecting humour and providing entertainment for children and adults alike. In a similar way any public facility connected with sport and leisure can employ such creativity, which might also encourage greater engagement.

Gardens for rehabilitation

Gardens are special places for many, and often harbour reflections and memories,

Inclusive gardens
—
Gardening can involve various low-impact activities, making it ideal even for people with physical limitations. Gardening is engaging, too, and brings communities together. Seating areas like this one by Zetterman Garden Design in Stockholm, Sweden enable everyone, not only those able to work in the garden, to participate in the space.

261

through their scents, sounds and visual and tactile qualities. Such gardens can be excellent for therapeutic purposes and healing, and may be used preventively or for rehabilitation.

When planning a garden for rehabilitation it is important to understand the needs of the intended users. There are always things going on in a garden, with many opportunities to carry out fulfilling tasks such as weeding, pruning, watering, harvesting, sweeping up leaves and feeding birds in winter. These tasks vary in length and intensity and can suit a range of individuals to provide exercise and encourage balance and coordination. In this way gardens can increase self-esteem and give people a sense of meaning through participation in the space.

Gardens are not only useful spaces for physical rehabilitation, but can promote a positive mental state and increase motivation. With things always changing and evolving, a garden inspires curiosity and expectations, which can distract from pain and other worries, or simply provide an escape from everyday life. Furthermore, gardens teach us to be patient: to sow seeds, to water the sprouts and then wait to see plants to bloom can be viewed as analogous to tracking individual human endeavour and results.

Senior living

What we choose to give priority to in life depends on many things, such as where in the world we live and our economic situation. If we have the option to do so, we might take charge of our wellness and our way of living. When getting older we might still be physically vital, and yet wish to downsize, feeling that the workload associated with a large house and a garden is too much. At this stage in life, moving to shared housing is an option for some, where there are common spaces and where neighbours know and care for one another. In some shared housing in Scandinavia, gardens

have become a focus, sometimes even acting as the main room where people meet on a daily basis. Regardless of age and personal interests, a shared garden can be a stimulating and uplifting place. It is a natural meeting point for activities or celebrations, or just a relaxed place in which to make conversation.

When planning a garden for the elderly, ergonomic aspects should be considered, to allow people to move around in the space easily. Reaching far up and down might prove difficult, so planting and edible crops should be planned to be within easy reach. Impaired senses might need to be worked around, with plants that flower in bright colours and carry large foliage, making them clearly visible. Many Scandinavians will recall childhoods and younger years spent in close contact with nature. The sound and feel of walking across gravel may remind them of a beach, and the smell of apples of an expansive orchard. Considering the endless positive, encouraging and uplifting qualities that a garden can provide, it should be everyone's right to have access to a garden or a green space, regardless of age or physical ability.

Gardens are freedom

Gardens are made to stay with us for decades; designing them represents freedom as well as responsibility – if we plan them with love and care, they should take care of us in return. And not only do they reward people, but they also give back to our wider environment. Scandinavia is a region of great freedom, and with continuous work in our gardens towards everything that we stand for and everything that we are, we will continue to demonstrate how much we appreciate our heritage and where we come from. To witness the beauty of grasses waving in the wind, or to take notice of the wings of a butterfly or the light reflected in a chunk of crystalline stone, is to feel the power of Mother Earth – and to us that is freedom.

Secure environments
—
Gardens are positive and motivating places, where training and play can take place without pressure. A garden, being a living space, always has something new to offer, and is a place to set aside worries and concerns. Integrating areas for different activities, interaction and play, such as in this senior living complex by Bovieran in Norrtälje, Sweden, naturally opens up opportunities for socializing with neighbours while feeling safe.

Inviting interaction
—
We sometimes see
gardens from different
elevations, for example
from tall buildings. This
large pool in a space in
Fornebu, Norway by
Bjørbekk & Lindheim
Landskapsarkitekter,
with stepping stones,
a wooden seating area
('the island') and a
fountain is visually
interesting from all levels.
The landscape balances
delicacy and strength
and invites interaction;
delicate ornamental
grasses and willow
trees are framed by strict
and solid corten steel,
and the same material
is used in a custom-
made barbecue as well
for the several seats for
relaxation. The landscape
is further enhanced by
lighting in the evenings,
with 'the island'
appearing to float.

Soft and comforting foliage
—

Left: The texture of a plant, and its shape and colour send particular messages. While a thistle signals to you to stay away with its sharp foliage, some grasses, like this *Stipa tenuissima* seem to send out a message of comfort. When designing with plants in places of healing, where trust and comfort are important, specimens that have a calming effect should be considered. In this garden by Bjørbekk & Lindheim Landskapsarkitekter in Fornebu, Norway, both the appearance and the feel of the *Stipa tenuissima* are soft, and this is even more pronounced when it is in bloom.

A welcoming space
—

Below: This residential area by Bjørbekk & Lindheim Landskapsarkitekter in Fornebu, Norway is situated next to a bay. Very early in the project a decision was made to reinforce the relationship with the sea, connecting residents with the water. Consequently, a canal was extended into the residential area. This inner part of the canal consists of shallow fresh water with elements inviting interaction with the space, such as a stepping stone path across the water. Small, welcoming trees, such as magnolias, Japanese Judas trees and cherries have been selected, as well as local plants such as willow, lilac, waxberries and juneberries.

Playing with scale
—
This playground
by MONSTRUM in
Stockholm, Sweden
uses scale and proportion
creatively, by magnifying
things found in the
wild. Two giant owls
rule the space, being
the tallest objects. Inside
the owls are stairs and
ladders to climb and
then to slide down
from. Lights have been
installed, making the
owls' eyes glow at night.
Next to the owls grows
a cluster of mushrooms,
incorporating ropes and
bars, and one in which
children can spin as
if in a carousel. Large-
scale ants are perfect
for smaller children to
balance on, marching
all over the playground
and painted colourfully
in pinks and reds.

Wooden adventure
—
In this playground by MONSTRUM in Stockholm, Sweden, all products are made from wood, handcrafted in Denmark, setting an example for playground best practice. The idea is to allow children to experience a sense of danger and feel the thrill of taking a chance, and landing on their feet again. Large oak leaf-plates are scattered around, just like in an autumn storm. Meanwhile the land of flower hammocks is not just about thrills, but also provides areas in which to rest and chat to friends. A flower sandpit is included for the youngest to enjoy. They might also be interested in the three acorns, which act as playhouses.

*Bold colours for visual
clarity*
—
When planning a garden
for the elderly, the brief
is likely to be somewhat
different than when
planning gardens for
young and middle-aged
people. In this greenhouse
garden by Bovieran in
Norrtälje, Sweden, filled
with exotics, vivid pink
bougainvillea and large
hibiscus flowers can be
found. A red bridge
provides a splash of
colour as a clear and
easy-to-see focal point
in stark contrast to the
lush green space.

Communal winter garden
—
This senior living complex by Bovieran in Norrtälje, Sweden has a central communal garden, created to reflect the vegetation of the French Riviera, despite the rain or snow outside the window. In such an enclosed winter garden, tropical plants such as palms, citrus trees, agave and bougainvillea can be enjoyed throughout the year, even in the darkest winter. The garden becomes a natural place to meet, with activities and various other events arranged throughout the week.

A venue for the arts
—
A garden in a city can offer the perfect venue for events, workshops and other entertainment, just like any other room. This garden by Gullik Gulliksen Landscape Architects in Skien, Norway is part of an exciting rejuvenation of an urban space, also containing a restaurant and café. The garden is open to all and is a popular venue. Bringing together the ideas of urban regeneration and public art involves forming a close collaboration with local renowned artists, who have contributed artworks to the space.

Light sculptures
—

Art in a garden can complement planting through its shapes and materials. This city oasis in Skien, Norway by Gullik Gulliksen Landscape Architects uses ornamental trees, grasses and bamboo alongside a collection of sculptural glass lamps. These sculptures, created by Tuva Gonsholt, are inspired by shapes found in nature. The idea behind the art is to express vigorous yet soft, feminine and elegant spheres, bursting with life. In the evening the glass sculptures give the garden a completely different look, acting like silent fireflies in the space.

Soothing, evocative wildlife
—

Using plants that attract wildlife into a garden – as here in Turku, Finland – can be uplifting and evoke precious memories for the elderly. To hear the soothing sounds of birds and other wildlife, and to see butterflies and other insects can be both relaxing and stimulating. In our very quiet Scandinavian winters, when most wildlife is asleep and birds have migrated or are hiding in the forest, they are all missed, and their return marks the longed-for change of the seasons.

Sculptural skate park
—
Sports and leisure facilities in gardens and landscapes are visually inviting and encourage an active lifestyle. This skate park by Janne Saario Landscape Architecture in Espoo, Finland demonstrates how public facilities – not necessarily used, but seen by everyone – can be built to create visual interest for all in the landscape. The design adapts to the granite rock, with a hand-shaped concrete surface that skirts around the shape of the rock on different levels. The rock works as a natural grandstand, enabling viewers to watch the action, and also creates interesting surfaces for skateboarding.

Integrated social space

—

Companies creating
outdoor spaces should
think about how these
can reflect their identity;
their values and beliefs.
This courtyard in
Stockholm, Sweden
by Zetterman Garden
Design was created
for the company that
managed the property,
a historical building,
with the aim of making
the space suitable as
a social area for staff
breaks and functions.
The design fully respects
and accentuates the style
and historical significance
of the building and
the interior. Traditional
granite and diabase
stone from the Swedish
west coast is used in
the design.

Delineating human space
—
Open overhead structures
are useful for imposing
a more human spatial
understanding on areas
of cities where houses
are tall. They make a
space feel more private,
but without feeling
enclosed or losing
views of sky, often
only glimpsed directly
above. This courtyard by
Zetterman Garden Design
in Stockholm, Sweden
uses a pergola of wrought
iron, which forms a strong
architectural element in
the space. Lighting gives
the courtyard a totally
different complexion at
night, and the emphasis
is moved away from
the pergola on to the
sculptural clipped trees.

Conservatory workspace
—

Modern living can be
hectic, creating stress
and a lack of balance.
Using a garden as a
workspace may help
counteract this, however.
Weather permitting, you
can use any space in
the garden as your office,
but a small building or
conservatory may be
most practical. This
conservatory by
Paradehusets Tegnestue/
Paradehuset Landscape
Design Studio in Midwest
Jutland, Denmark is
a great example of a
multipurpose space,
perfect to relax in,
with subtropical plants
boosting the creative
ambiance. Of course
you can get distracted
when working in a
garden, just like in any
other place. The difference
is, in a garden, you
only get distracted by
beautiful things.

Private and public
—
Good communication between private and communal areas of a garden encourages people to interact, as well as providing privacy when desired, as shown in this project by ARKÍS arkitektar in Egilsstadir, Iceland. Each of the four flats in this building has a private garden, with a patio directly connected to the living room – connecting interior and exterior – and out on to the common spaces. Emphasis is placed on good visual connections within the garden. The private gardens have a larch patio, which includes a simple yet striking vertical climbing frame for a green wall in summer, as well as berry shrubs close by. The patio also includes a bird bath and light fixtures that allow residents to enjoy the garden from inside the house at night.

Soothing water

—
Water in a garden can exert a strong sensory influence on feelings and mood. Water can also distract from undesirable background noise. In this garden by Zetterman Garden Design in Kalmar, Sweden the water feature has different settings, from a solid flow to jumping jets, and its height can also be adjusted. Alternatively, it can be completely switched off.

*Encouraging movement
and use*
—

This house and garden
by ARKÍS arkitektar in
Egilsstadir, Iceland is
designed as a home for
four disabled people,
and is designed to
encourage both residents
and employees to use
the garden for exercise.
One of the main design
concepts was to create
opportunities for residents
to enjoy the garden in all
seasons, with easy access
through the garden and
a hot tub and fireplace
in the common outdoor
area. The material palette
for the scheme uses
Icelandic vegetation and
trees, both deciduous
trees and conifers, with
larch used as cladding
and on the common
patio.

Versatile courtyard
—
Courtyards are common
in Scandinavian cities,
working as 'green lungs'
and accommodating
people and wildlife. This
garden by Zetterman
Garden Design in
Stockholm, Sweden
was designed as a space
for the residents of the
adjacent building, and
incorporates several
seating areas, with
smaller individual spaces
as well as larger areas
for bigger groups. Hedges
work as partition walls
between these areas,
providing the garden
with as much green as
possible, and forming
more restful spaces.
A barbecue comes into
play in summer, as well
as a sandpit for the
youngest residents.

Plants in schemes for the elderly should be considered in terms of foliage, size, fragrance and colour. Smells should be gentle and kept at a distance from any seating areas, and colours should be bright so they seem to come forward. Warm colours such as pinks, reds, oranges and yellows as well as large flower heads are highly visible. To grow flowers that quickly show results is most uplifting and communicates vitality, such as these radiant, vibrant sunflowers in Stockholm, Sweden. Recognizable for its large flower heads and warm colours, this tall annual is easy to grow as long as it gets enough sun.

Far left: An outdoor shower placed in a hidden corner is free to use for any of the residents.

Left: Concrete stools are both useful and fulfil a decorative purpose.

Below: *Miscanthus sinensis* is a valuable addition to this roof terrace, displaying shiny red plumes.

Opposite: An overhead structure covered in climbers provides excellent shade once the sun gets too intense on the terrace.

Plant list
—

*Calamagrostis ×
acutiflora* 'Karl Foerster'

Fargesia murielae

Miscanthus sinensis

Hosta fortunei

Iris germanica

Hedera helix

Parthenocissus inserta

Hydrangea anomala
subsp. *petiolaris*

Rosa helenae 'Lykkefund'

Making the most of a tight urban space in Oslo

—

Oslo, Norway
Design by: Gullik Gulliksen
Landscape Architects
245m²

Roof terraces often have to accommodate pipes, ventilation shafts and other utilities, which necessitates extra-cautious planning and creative solutions. This site is a narrow but deep strip between two party walls. The roof terrace sits on a building comprising nine flats in downtown Oslo, Norway. The developer's brief for this roof was to regenerate the space and give meaning to difficult areas.

The approach and main focus for this roof was to maximize the outdoor experience for as many of the residents as possible, so they could use the terrace at the same time without causing any disturbance. Despite the site being spatially compact the entire terrace is exposed to the sun, so it can get very warm and dry, particularly during summer, which is much appreciated by the residents but requires planning for plants.

To make an interesting yet intimate space on the terrace, each void was given its own function, yet the visual expression is consistent throughout the space. A larger space is given over to a dining area with space for up to fifteen people to enjoy at the same time. The area is covered with a pergola over which plants climb, filtering the light and making the dining experience more comfortable. Other areas vary in size and have been created for reflection and lounging, all containing planting for a lush and relaxed ambience. The air in Oslo and many other parts of Scandinavia is generally dry, with little humidity in summer, and many of us enjoy an outdoor shower to cool off in summer, so one is included here against one of the taller walls on the terrace.

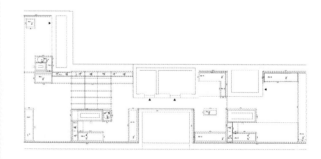

Heat-treated pine was used throughout the entire terrace, for flooring and walls as well as in bespoke structures such as furniture and planters. Not only is wood a soft and comfortable material to walk across, often perceived as caring and gentle, but functionally it is very durable and light in weight. The choice of using heat-treated wood, free from chemical additives, makes the terrace both environmental friendly and natural in appearance.

Index of plants

—

Annuals

Atriplex hortensis purpurea, 33, 183
Eruca sativa, 249
Gentiana nivalis, 169
Lactuca sativa var. capitate, 249
Lactuca sativa var. longifolia, 249
Papaver somniferum 'Claus Dalby', 116

Climbers

Clematis montana, 188
Clematis 'Mrs T. Lundell' E, 131
Clematis 'Nelly Moser', 131
Clematis 'Paul Farges', 170
Clematis 'Riga', 205
Clematis tangutica, 125
Clematis 'Violet Purple' E, 205
Hedera helix, 283
Hedera helix 'Baltica', 39
Hydrangea petiolaris, 216, 283
Lonicera periclymenum, 105
Parthenocissus, 218
Parthenocissus inserta, 283
Rosa 'Ghislaine de Féligonde', 99

Conifers

Juniperus communis 'Hibernica', 79
Picea, 169
Picea abies 'Little Gem', 79
Pinus, 169
Pinus mugo, 257
Pinus mugo var. pumilio, 195
Pinus mugo 'Mops', 205
Pinus parviflora 'Shirobana', 205
Pinus sylvestris, 200, 257
Taxus, 192
Taxus baccata, 39, 229
Thuja occidentalis 'Brabant', 200
Thuja occidentalis 'Danica', 257
Thuja occidentalis 'Fastigiata', 257

Grasses

Briza media, 182
Calamagrostis, 46
Calamagrostis × acutiflora 'Overdam', 79
Calamagrostis × acutiflora 'Karl Foerster', 39, 156, 283
Carex elata aurea, 76
Carex morrowii variegata, 229
Cynosurus cristatus, 78
Deschampsia cespitosa 'Bronzeschleier', 79, 119
Deschampsia cespitosa 'Goldtau', 99
Festuca cinerea, 257
Festuca gautieri, 39, 71
Festuca glauca 'Intense Blue', 85
Helictotrichon pubescens, 78
Imperata cylindrica 'Red Baron', 229
Leymus arenarius 'Blue Dune', 85
Miscanthus, 44, 46, 75, 205
Miscanthus sinensis, 282, 283
Miscanthus sinensis 'Dronning Ingrid', 99
Miscanthus sinensis 'Nishidake', 171
Molinia caerulea ssp. arundinacea 'Transparent', 131
Molina caerulea 'Variegata', 79
Pennisetum, 75
Phalaris arundinacea 'Picta', 257

Phyllostachys aureosulcata 'Spectabilis', 71
Sesleria, 205
Sesleria nitida, 33, 131
Stipa tenuissima, 93, 265

Perennials

Achillea filipendulina 'Parker's Variety', 99, 118
Achillea millefolium 'Terracotta', 88
Achillea millefolium 'Red Velvet', 124
Actaea simplex 'Brunette', 80, 171
Alchemilla, 45
Alchemilla mollis, 85, 96
Allium, 174
Allium Christophii, 131
Allium 'Purple Sensation', 33
Anemone hupehensis 'Splendens', 99
Anemone x hybrida 'Honorine Jobert', 46
Anthriscus sylvestris 'Ravenswing', 123
Aquilegia chrysantha 'Yellow Queen', 100
Aquilegia 'Nora Barlow', 99
Aquilegia vulgaris var. stellata 'Black Barlow', 93
Armeria maritima, 54
Artemisia, 45
Artemisia 'Powis Castle', 2, 4
Artemisia ludoviciana 'Silver Queen', 87
Artemisia stelleriana 'Morris Form', 99
Asarum europaeum, 44
Astilbe, 75
Astilbe arendsii 'Fanal', 257
Astilbe arendsii 'Weisse Gloria', 257
Astrantia major, 131
Astrantia major 'Claret', 99
Astrantia major 'Roma', 80
Brunnera macrophylla 'Betty Bowring', 108
Brunnera macrophylla 'Dawson's White', 44
Brunnera macrophylla 'Mr Morse', 96
Calamintha nepeta, 131
Campanula, 105
Campanula carpatica 'White Clips', 257
Campanula persicifolia, 78
Campanula rotundifolia, 77
Catanache caerulea, 33
Centaurea jacea, 78
Cerastium, 45
Cerastium tomentosum, 195
Chamerion angustifolium, 77
Crambe maritima, 85
Dicentra spectabilis 'Alba', 99
Echinacea 'Green Jewel', 131
Echinacea 'Sunrise', 99
Echinacea 'Sunset', 99
Echinacea purpurea, 105
Echinacea purpurea 'Green Envy', 2, 4
Echinacea purpurea 'Magnus', 115, 128
Echinacea purpurea 'Pica Bella', 128
Echinacea purpurea 'Tomato Soup', 99
Echinops bannaticus, 75
Echinops ritro 'Veitch's Blue', 127
Echinops sphaerocephalus 'Arctic Glow', 111
Epimediumx perralchicum 'Frohnleiten', 80
Eryngium, 75
Eryngium planum, 83
Eupatorium maculatum 'Album', 183
Galium verum, 78

Geranium renardii, 165
Geranium 'Rozanne', 124
Geranium sanguineum 'Apfelblüte', 131, 170
Geum chiloense 'Mrs Bradshaw', 99, 100, 101
Geum rivale, 77
Helenium 'Rubinzwerg', 118
Helleborus orientalis 'Pink Lady', 99
Hemerocallis 'Green Flutter', 87
Hemerocallis 'Joan Senior', 131
Hemerocallis 'Pardon Me', 80, 99, 124
Hemerocallis 'Pink Damask', 99
Hemerocallis 'Stafford', 115
Hemerocallis 'Stella d'Oro', 170
Hemerocallis lilioasphodelus, 105
Heuchera, 174
Heuchera 'Beauty Color', 99
Heuchera 'Chocolate Ruffles', 80
Heuchera 'Marmalade' PBR, 99
Heuchera micrantha 'Palace Purple', 99
Hosta, 174
Hosta 'Cherry Berry', 99
Hosta 'Frances Williams, 131
Hosta fortunei, 283
Hosta fortunei 'Patriot', 44, 77, 96, 283
Hosta sieboldiana 'Elegans', 165
Hylotelephium sieboldii, 221, 229
Iris 'Carnaby', 115
Iris germanica, 283
Iris germanica 'Apricot Silk', 99
Iris germanica 'Ola Kala', 99
Iris germanica 'Superstition', 99
Iris sibirica, 165
Iris sibirica 'Perry's Blue', 88
Iris sibirica 'Shirley Pope', 257
Iris variegata, 76
Knautia arvensis, 78, 104
Knautia macedonica, 104, 118
Knautia macedonica 'Mars Midget', 99
Kniphofia 'Alcazar', 121
Ligularia dentate 'Desdemona', 75
Lilium 'Golden Splendour', 99
Lilium 'Landini', 105
Lilium martagon, 85
Lilium martagon var. album, 165
Lotus corniculatus, 78
Lupinus polyphyllus, 107
Meconopsis betonicifolia, 93
Nepeta x faassenii 'Walker's Low', 88
Nepeta racemosa 'Superba', 108, 131
Paeonia lactiflora 'Buckeye Belle', 99
Paeonia lactiflora 'Coral Charm', 105
Paeonia lactiflora 'Karl Rosenfield', 99
Paeonia lactiflora 'Pink Hawaiian Coral', 99
Paeonia lactiflora 'Sarah Bernhardt', 257
Paeonia mascula, 126
Papaver orientale, 46
Papaver orientale 'Beauty of Livermere', 105
Papaver pseudo-orientale, 115
Persicaria affinis 'Superba' (Polygonum), 99
Persicaria amplexicaulis 'Alba', 96
Persicaria polymorpha, 116
Potentilla x tonguei, 112
Phlomis, 75
Phlomis russeliana, 119

Designers

Photo credits

—

Front cover: Marianne Folling (photo) tuja66/Alamy Stock Photo (background)
Back cover, top row: Annika Zetterman, Østengen og Bergo Landskapsarkitekter, Pia Enghild
Back cover, bottom row: Annika Zetterman

2 Marianne Folling; 7 Annika Zetterman; 8 Pernille Kaalund; 11–14 Annika Zetterman; 15 Torfi Agnarsson; 16 Andreas von Gegerfelt; 17 Markus Linderoth; 18 Østengen og Bergo Landskapsarkitekter; 20–21 Markus Linderoth; 22 Annika Zetterman; 23 Åke E:son Lindman; 24a Annika Zetterman; 24b Gullik Gulliksen Landscape Architects; 25 Annika Zetterman; 26–27 Åke E:son Lindman; 28 Annika Zetterman; 29 Magnus Ekström; 30 Pia Enghild; 31 Jørgen Larsen; 32 Marianne Folling; 33 Annika Zetterman; 34a Gregory Bryan Kobett/ Paradehusets Landscape Design Studio; 34b Gullik Gulliksen Landscape Architects; 35a Gregory Bryan Kobett/Paradehusets Landscape Design Studio; 35b Arne Thomsen; 36 Annika Zetterman; 37 Espen Grønli; 38–41 Markus Linderoth; 44 Annika Zetterman; 45 Pernille Kaalund; 46 Annika Zetterman; 47 Roger Gehrman; 48–50 Annika Zetterman; 51 Nils Petter Dale; 52a Gregory Bryan Kobett/ Paradehusets Landscape Design Studio; 52b Gullik Gulliksen Landscape Architects; 53 Kasper Dudzik; 54 Annika Zetterman; 55 Torfi Agnarsson; 56–57 Åke E:son Lindman; 58 Pia Enghild; 59–60 Annika Zetterman; 61–62 Pia Enghild; 63 Annika Zetterman; 64–65 Pia Enghild; 66 Markus Linderoth; 67 Gullik Gulliksen Landscape Architects; 68a Annika Zetterman; 68b Gullik Gulliksen Landscape Architects; 69 Pernille Kaalund; 70–71 Pernille Kaalund; 74 Kjeld Slot; 75 Annika Zetterman; 76 Kjeld Slot; 77 Marianne Folling; 78–81 Annika Zetterman; 82–83 Marianne Folling; 84a Kjeld Slot; 84b Marianne Folling; 85 Annika Zetterman; 86–87a Annika Zetterman; 87b Østengen og Bergo landskapsarkitekter; 88–89 Marianne Folling; 90–92 Annika Zetterman; 93 Darren Saines Hagedesign AS; 94–95 Marianne Folling; 96a Annika Zetterman; 96b Marianne Folling; 97 Arne Thomsen; 98–108 Annika Zetterman; 109–111 Marianne Folling; 112–115 Annika Zetterman; 116–117 Marianne Folling; 118 Annika Zetterman; 119 Kjeld Slot; 120–121 Annika Zetterman; 122–123 Marianne Folling; 124–127 Annika Zetterman; 128–129 Marianne Folling; 130–133 Annika Zetterman; 137 Birgir Teitsson; 138–140 Annika Zetterman; 141 Marianne Folling; 142 Markus Linderoth; 143 Dag G. Nordsveen; 144 Jamie Bell; 145 John Robert Nilsson Arkitektkontor; 146 Annika Zetterman; 147 Pia Enghild; 148 Marianne Folling; 149 Annika Zetterman; 150 Suvi Tuokko; 151 Kim Ahm; 152 Jamie Bell; 153 Gullik Gulliksen Landscape Architects; 154–156 Annika Zetterman; 157 Dag G. Nordsveen; 158 Annika Zetterman; 159 Suvi Tuokko; 160 Torfi Agnarsson; 161 Suvi Tuokko; 162a Heidi Hannus; 162b Annika Zetterman; 163 Tor Haddeland; 164–165 Gullik Gulliksen Landscape Architects; 168 Annika Zetterman; 170 Åke E:son Lindman; 171–174 Annika Zetterman; 175 Birgir Teitsson; 176 Nils Petter Dale; 177 Annika Zetterman; 178–179 Kasper Dudzik; 180–181a Annika Zetterman; 181b Gregory Bryan Kobett/Paradehusets Landscape Design Studio; 182a Annika Zetterman; 182b–185 Marianne Folling; 186 Annika Zetterman; 187a Pia Enghild; 187b Annika Zetterman; 188 Marianne Folling; 189 Annika Zetterman; 190–192a Marianne Folling; 192b–193 Annika Zetterman; 194–197 Annika Zetterman; 200 Heidi Hannus; 201 Pia Enghild; 202–203 Annika Zetterman; 205 Gullik Gulliksen Landscape Architects; 206–207 Pia Enghild; 208–209 Annika Zetterman; 210 Pia Enghild; 211 Markus Linderoth; 212al Heidi Hannus; 212br Annika Zetterman; 213 Suvi Tuokko; 214–215 Markus Linderoth; 216 Pia Enghild; 217 Åke E:son Lindman; 218 Annika Zetterman; 219 Annika Zetterman; 220 Pia Enghild; 221 Åke E:son Lindman; 222–223 Annika Zetterman; 224–226 Bruce Damonte; 227 Gullik Gulliksen Landscape Architects; 228 Pia Enghild; 232 Annika Zetterman; 233 Gregory Bryan Kobett/ Paradehusets Landscape Design Studio; 235 Hans Zetterman; 236 Annika Zetterman; 238–241 Klas Sjöberg; 242 Gregory Bryan Kobett/ Paradehusets Landscape Design Studio; 243–245 Annika Zetterman; 246 Østengen og Bergo landskapsarkitekter; 247 Annika Zetterman; 248 Henri Vettenranta; 249a Jørgen Larsen; 249b Annika Zetterman; 250–251 Annika Zetterman; 252a Cory Benford Brown; 252b Hans Zetterman; 253–255 Annika Zetterman; 256–257 Suvi Tuokko; 260–261 Annika Zetterman; 263 Martin Borgs Wannborga; 264–265 Bjørbekk & Lindheim Landskapsarkitekter; 266–269 Annika Zetterman; 270–271 Camilla Jensen; 272 Gullik Gulliksen Landscape Architects; 272b Annika Zetterman; 273 Janne Saario; 274–275 Annika Zetterman; 276 Gregory Bryan Kobett/Paradehusets Landscape Design Studio; 277a Birgir Teitsson; 277b Annika Zetterman; 278–279 Sigurgeir Sigurjonsson; 280–281 Annika Zetterman; 282–283 Gullik Gulliksen Landscape Architects

Acknowledgments

—

This book is the result of an idea that has been with me for more than ten years, working as a garden designer in Sweden and abroad. Spending many years overseas, I was often asked what characterized a current Scandinavian garden and how we, as design nations, translated our values into our outdoor environments. I would like to thank everyone for asking these questions; without them, and without my years abroad, this book would not have been conceived.

My deepest appreciation and acknowledgment goes to all architects, landscape architects, garden designers, artists, photographers and contributors to this book. Your creative work, your views and your participation is what made the creation of this book possible.

I would like to express my gratitude to collaborators and clients whose trust, knowledge and positive outlook have played an important role in creating this book. Special recognition goes to Patrik Windisch and Andreas Eneskjöld, who have paved the way for many of my creative endeavours; Marléne Måbrink, for your generosity and valuable comments about plants; Andrew Fisher Tomlin, for my early, invaluable experience and fun times at your design practice in London.

I am grateful for the unfailing support and interest shown by my parents, brother and friends: my dear friend and artistic companion Linda Lampenius Cullberg, with whom I have bounced off feelings and thoughts through the process of writing. Duncan Greenaway, for our years in London and your infectious enthusiasm about architecture; you are a true inspiration every day. Paul Southouse, thank you for telling me to never change, making me express who I am in the book. A special mention goes to Feroz Gajia and Laura Willis, who put me in contact with Thames & Hudson.

Last but not least I wish to extend my sincere thanks to my publisher Thames & Hudson. I owe a debt of gratitude to commissioning editor Lucas Dietrich for adopting and accepting my idea. Thanks to Bethany Wright for your efficient and helpful approach during the process of putting the book together. To everyone involved in the editing process whose effort and impressive work gives the book its character, thank you.